FRANCIS SCHAEFFER

FRANCIS SCHAEFFER

Mostyn Roberts

PUBLISHING WITH A MISSION

EP BOOKS
Faverdale North
Darlington
DL3 0PH, England

e-mail: sales@epbooks.org

web: http://www.epbooks.org

First published 2012

British Library Cataloguing in Publication Data available

ISBN-13: 978-085234-792-8   ISBN-10: 0-85234-792-8

Printed and bound in Great Britain by MPG Books Group, Bodmin and King's Lynn.

CONTENTS

Francis and Edith Schaeffer in the 1970s

Notes to the reader

1. The subject of this biography is variously called Fran, Francis, Schaeffer or Francis Schaeffer depending on what seems natural in the context.

2. In line with the nature of this series, to avoid footnotes and clogging the text with references, I have generally given detailed references only where the source is not referred to in 'Further reading'. References to:

   'Colin Duriez' or 'Duriez' are to his book, *Francis Schaeffer: An Authentic Life*;

   'Jerram Barrs', to his Covenant Seminary Lectures, *Francis Schaeffer, The Early Years* and *The Later Years*;

   'Edith' or *The Tapestry* to that book except where otherwise indicated.

   References to Schaeffer's works are often given in the form '(CW 3:305)', which means *The Complete Works of Francis Schaeffer*, volume 3, page 305.

   Full details of these works are in 'Further reading'.

3. I am very grateful to Ranald Macaulay of Christian Heritage, Cambridge, and Andrew Fellows of L'Abri, Greatham, Hampshire, for reading my manuscript and making many helpful suggestions and corrections; and to my wife, Hilary, who read it all through to sift for more mistakes. The responsibility for the contents of the book is, of course, entirely mine.

4. I would also like to express thanks to Crossway for permission to use the photo of Francis Schaeffer on the front cover and that of him with Edith in the front of the book.

PREFACE

'Bought a book for 10p in a sale — *Escape from Reason...*' So reads an entry in my diary for May 1975. During a 'gap year' as a language assistant in Brittany, France, I was on a short break in London. I found myself in a bookshop near Oxford Circus. The title, *Escape from Reason*, appealed to me. Rather too influenced by certain French authors in my 'A' level studies, I was leaning towards the idea that existence was meaningless. Rebellion against reason seemed both attractive and noble. I even fixed posters in my room upside down — after all, why not? In the end, did it make any difference, if life was absurd? (Later on, I realized Schaeffer would have gently pointed out: 'But you could not fix them in mid-air'. There are strict limits to our power to rebel against the reality of things.) French students found it amusing; I explained to them that it was their writers who had inspired me. Ideas have consequences.

A book promising further 'escape from reason' was, therefore, just up my street. Francis Schaeffer? Never heard of him, but it was an interesting name.

Reading that book did not make me a Christian, but it was a turning point. It was, of course, the opposite of what I had expected. I do not suppose I understood much of the detail of Schaeffer's argument, but from seeing only disjointedness in life, I came to see a basic unity in things. The key behind that unity was the existence of God and the fact that he had created all things.

Five months later, in my first term at university, I became a Christian. It would be five years before I read anything else by Schaeffer. That too was a major growth-point in my life.

Let me now introduce you to this remarkable man, Francis Schaeffer, whose ministry and writings have been a source of enlightenment and encouragement to many people throughout the world over the last sixty years, and whose voice deserves to continue to be heard.

CHRONOLOGY

1947	Travelled through Europe for three months to evaluate state of Christianity in Europe
1948	Family moved to Lausanne, Switzerland, as missionaries
1949	To Chalet des Frênes, Champéry
1951	Spiritual crisis in the winter months
1952	August — Francis August Schaeffer V ('Franky') born
1953	Returned to U.S. on furlough
1953–54	Travelled across America, speaking 346 times in 515 days. His main series of talks became *True Spirituality*
1954	May — awarded honorary Doctor of Divinity degree by Highland College
1954	September — returned to Champéry. Franky contracted polio
1955	February — received notice to leave Switzerland
1955	April — moved into Chalet les Mélèzes, Huémoz
1955	May — recognized as the beginning of 'L'Abri' at Huémoz
1955	4 June — resigned from Independent Board for Presbyterian Foreign Missions
1958	English L'Abri founded
1968	Published *Escape from Reason* and *The God Who is There*
1971	June — received honorary Doctor of Letters degree from Gordon College, Wenham, Massachusetts
1972	Published *He Is There And He Is Not Silent*
1974	Began work on *How Should We Then Live?* film series

1977	22-city seminar and speaking tour in connection with the series
1977	Helped to found the International Council on Biblical Inerrancy
1977	Began work on *Whatever Happened to the Human Race?* with 'Chuck' Koop
1978	October — diagnosed with lymphoma at Mayo Clinic, Rochester, Minnesota
1979	September — speaking tour for *Whatever Happened to the Human Race?*
1979	American HQ of L'Abri established at Rochester
1982	Publication of *The Complete Works of Francis Schaeffer*
1983	Received honorary Doctor of Laws degree from the Simon Greenleaf School of Law
1983	December — flown in critical condition from Switzerland to Mayo Clinic
1984	March-April — seminar tour of Christian colleges in connection with his last book, *The Great Evangelical Disaster*
1984	15 May — died at his home in Rochester

1

THE EARLY YEARS

In her account of the early life of Francis Schaeffer in *The Tapestry*, his wife, Edith, tells us that the doctor who attended his birth was 'rip-roaringly drunk'. He managed to tie a sheet to the bed and told Bessie, Francis' mother, to pull on the sheet and 'push'. The procedure worked, for Bessie later recounted: 'It was easy. I just pulled on the sheet and pushed, and the baby was there on the bed!'

Unfortunately, the doctor was not sober enough to remember to register the birth. This was discovered when Francis applied for his first passport in 1947. Bessie was still alive and able to swear before a notary that Francis August Schaeffer IV had been born on 30 January 1912.

Francis was of German stock on his father's side, his grandfather Franz August Schaeffer having emigrated to America and settled in Germantown, Pennsylvania, in 1869. Franz was killed in an accident while working on the railroad in 1879, leaving a three-year-old son, Francis August Schaeffer III ('Frank'). Frank's was a hard childhood, and by the age of eleven, after very little schooling, he had to work sorting coal to help the family income. In his early teens, he ran away to sea; his seafaring experience included serving in the Spanish-American war of 1898. He later worked in a steelworks in Germantown.

In time, young Frank met Bessie Williamson, born in 1880, also of Germantown, granddaughter on her mother's side of one William Joyce who had emigrated from England in 1846. Bessie's own father died when she was eight, and her childhood too was hard as she helped her mother make a living from taking in laundry. She vowed she would 'never be a slave to bringing up children'. Frank and Bessie married. Francis was their only child.

Frank had been an attender at his local Lutheran church as a boy but got little from it apart from a contempt for ministers: the pastor 'didn't know what work was; he just stood up there and talked'. Bessie attended an Evangelical Free Church, but she too derived little spiritual benefit. Frank was a conscientious man, hard-working and dedicated in his youth to helping out his mother financially. Before his marriage, he saved carefully to provide a home for his bride, while still sending money to his mother. Bessie, meanwhile, kept the house spotlessly clean, but there was a certain bitterness about her, no doubt fostered by childhood experiences. In later life she went to live with her son and his family in Switzerland and became a Christian. The home into which Francis was born, however, had nothing in the way of spiritual life or encouragement.

Neither was there anything in the way of academic or cultural stimulation in Francis' boyhood; after all, his parents had had none. There were no reading times, no pets or picnics, and few playmates were allowed to visit the house. In winter there was the Mummer's Parade to look forward to, and in summer a trip to the beach at Atlantic City. Frank was intent on his son being a manual worker and taught him carpentry and other manual skills. At school Francis recorded the second highest intelligence in twenty years, but no one at home told him. His parents did apparently at one time consider sending him to a private school, Germantown Academy, but nothing came of it.

When he went to Roosevelt Junior High School at age eleven, it was natural for Francis to choose subjects that would not take him in the direction of college — mechanical drawing, woodwork, electrical construction and metal work. At the same school, however, a teacher, Mrs Lidie Bell, 'opened the door', as he later put it, to the world of art. This was an interest that would never leave him. As a boy scout he was awarded the 'Pyramid Club Four Minute Speech Contest' cup in 1923. At this time he began attending the First Presbyterian Church of Germantown because of its association with the scout troop. Francis also had his first taste of classical music when he heard Tchaikovsky's '1812 Overture' played at an electrical show at the City Auditorium and heard the same piece again on the radio a few days later.

There were, therefore, glimmers of cultural light entering Francis' world, along with the plumbing, building, floor-laying and other skills his father was teaching him and by which he intended the young lad's future to be formed. Saturday jobs also educated him in the world of work. At seventeen, he took a job on a fish wagon, but it ended when he became disgusted with the way the boss treated his horse. Other jobs included work at a meat market, descaling the inside of a steam boiler with hammer and chisel, delivering ice and making beaded flowers and selling them from door to door.

It was of his father that Francis was thinking much later in life when he said that philosophical questions are not just for 'intellectuals'. 'Working people' had the same questions

though they expressed them differently. His father was
an intelligent man. He thought about life; he had just not
had the opportunities that came to rich people and to later
generations. There were many benefits, too, that Francis
gained from his home background. Jerram Barrs suggests at
least the following: an ease in relating to ordinary people; a
strong sense of the dignity of ordinary working people — as
he would say in one of his best-known sermons, there are
'no little people' in God's sight; a commitment to hard work,
whatever sort of work it was; a readiness to 'pitch in' and
help wherever needed; and a certain obstinacy of character
(which had its good and bad sides).

The door on culture was to swing further open when a
Sunday School teacher found him a job helping a Russian
count to learn English. The count's idea was to learn from a
biography of Catherine the Great, but Francis soon decided
another approach was needed. He went to a bookshop in
Philadelphia and asked for a beginner's English reading
book. He never ceased to be amazed at the providence of
God that sent him home with the wrong book — one on
Greek philosophy.

As he began reading, a love affair with philosophy
began — he felt he had 'come home'. What he found as he
read was that the questions on basic philosophical issues
far outstripped the answers. As he went to church, out of
convention, he realized the same thing was happening
— questions came from the pulpit under the influence
of critical, liberal theology, but no answers. Schaeffer
wondered if he should stop calling himself a Christian and
discard the Bible. He then faced the fact that he had never
read the whole Bible in his life and decided to read some of
it alongside Ovid night by night. Gradually, Ovid was set

aside, and the reading of the Bible was completed in about six months. He was seventeen. He read it as he would have read any other book; after all, who was there to teach him otherwise?

What he found was that the questions raised by the philosophers were answered by the Bible. He saw the interconnections between the worldview of philosophy and the worldview of the Bible. 'What rang the bell for me', he would say towards the end of his life, 'was the answers in Genesis, and that with these you really had answers — real answers — and without these there were no answers either in philosophy or in the religion I had heard preached.' Sometime in the next six months, he became a Christian, accepting Christ as his Saviour, having come to his understanding directly from the Word of God itself. By 3 September 1930, he could write in his diary, 'All truth is from the Bible'. He thought he had discovered something no one else knew. He did not at first call himself a Christian because he thought Christianity was the unreal stuff he had at church. For him, what he had discovered was a whole new way of looking at life.

That summer he finished at high school. His father gave him a 'Model A' Ford, and he began to look for a job. One hot August day in 1930, depressed and lonely, he was walking down Germantown Avenue, the main street, when he came across an evangelistic campaign tent. He went inside and was gripped by the fiery preaching. Here was the Christianity he had come to believe being preached by someone else. At the invitation he went forward (he was a bit confused by the terminology the evangelist, Anthony Zeoli, used, but he went nonetheless) and went home with a singing heart. He wrote in his diary:

19 August 1930 – Tent Meeting, Anthony Zeoli – have
decided to give my whole life to Christ unconditionally.

He went back to the tent meeting in the week, taking people
with him.

The mode of Schaeffer's conversion laid foundations
for major elements in his later ministry. There was the
emphasis on the Bible as truth, a conviction he held firmly
and preached tirelessly to the end, his last book, *The Great
Evangelical Disaster*, being an impassioned warning to
evangelicals against abandoning biblical inerrancy. This
conviction was strengthened by his spiritual crisis in
1950–1951, to which we shall come later. There is also the
conviction that the Bible really does have the answers to
philosophical questions. This is not at all to say he saw the
Bible merely as a book of philosophy, or that he approached
it in a philosophical way (particularly as philosophy is
commonly understood, entailing the exaltation of reason
above revelation), but he saw in Scripture profound answers
to life's big questions. In addition, there is the particular
attachment to the book of Genesis with its revelation of God
as Creator and the account of creation that was so central to
Schaeffer's analysis of worldviews and his understanding of
Christianity. Finally, there is in his early Christian experience
the passionate preaching of the gospel at the tent meeting,
the commitment to serve Christ and the desire to see people
saved. These qualities are present throughout his life.

Now, however, Schaeffer's life began to get complicated.
The destiny to which he had been working had been to
prepare to work with his hands, and so he enrolled in
September 1930 at the Drexel Institute for the night school
in Mechanical Engineering. This enabled him to work by

day, and for a month he earned thirty-two cents an hour doing assembly line work at RCA Victor. This came to an end when the bosses introduced an unjust system of double pay for more work for men but not for women, of whom there were many. One woman eventually snapped and shouted, 'Strike, strike'. After a little ensuing confusion, Schaeffer himself leapt onto a counter and shouted, 'Strike, strike' in support. He could, he said later, in different circumstances have become a 'labour organizer'.

Other jobs followed but, meanwhile, he had been talking to a Sunday School teacher and the headmaster of Germantown Academy about the possibility of going to college. The place recommended was Hampden-Sydney College in Virginia. The reason for this was that he was feeling the stirrings of a call to the ministry — to make known the God of whom he had become convinced and the Christ who was his Saviour. In his diary we read:

> 10 December 1930: Prayed with Sam Chestnut today.
> Now my mind is fully made up, I shall give my life to God's service.

Hampden-Sydney would be the preparation for studying theology.

There was, of course, the little question of what his parents would think about this. They considered ministers to be useless 'drones' and certainly did not want their son to be one. We have an idea of their reaction from other diary entries:

> 14 December: Mother and dad still hostile to my plan.
> I hope guidance comes strongly and surely.

15 December: Worried all day over mother and dad's *not* being back of me for my life's work. Decided to leave all to God.

16 December: Talked to dad alone, he said to go ahead and that mother would get over it.

In January 1931 he switched to Central High School evening school and studied Latin and German — quite an achievement given his dyslexia, which was not recognized as such at the time. By the summer he was ready to begin his studies at Hampden-Sydney. He had no idea as yet how he would pay his fees of $600 a year. The morning for his departure arrived. The night before, his father had instructed him to get up to see him before he went to work. Francis was up at 5.30am. 'I don't want a son who is a minister, and — I don't want you to go,' said his father, looking straight at him. After a silence, Francis said, 'Pop, give me a few minutes to go down to the cellar to pray'. His thoughts in disarray, tears falling, he prayed about the agonizing choice he had to make — his calling or his parents. In desperation, he resorted to the kind of prayer he would later advise people not to make. He asked God to show him by his tossing a coin: if the answer was 'heads' he would go. Heads it was. Not content, he said that if it was 'tails' next, he would go. Tails. Again, asking God to be patient with him, he said that if the third toss came up heads, he would go. Heads.

Returning to his father upstairs, Francis told him, 'Dad, I've *got* to go'. His father pushed past him, slamming the front door shut. Just before it shut, however, Francis heard him say, 'I'll pay for the first half year'.

Francis was off to college.

2

COLLEGE AND MARRIAGE

Schaeffer often said in later years that he regarded the confrontation at the door with his father as a step on the road to his father's conversion. That, however, was many years away. Now he had plenty to think about as he set off for Virginia. The previous day he had packed his belongings in a wooden, grey-painted box, screwed down at the corners. He had packed, among other things, his knee-length school breeches, or 'knickers', which he found comfortable. He later took to wearing similar breeches in Switzerland after the example of his son-in-law John Sandri. They became something of a hallmark.

He drove the 300 miles to Hampden-Sydney, about sixty miles south west of Richmond, in his 'Model A' Ford; Charlie Hoffman, a friend of his, went with him to drive the car back. Hampden-Sydney is one of the oldest colleges in the United States, founded in 1775. Schaeffer was delighted by its architecture, lawns and woods, but not happy to be placed in the Fourth Passage of Cushing Hall, renowned to be tough on freshmen (that is, new students). All the light bulbs in the staircase had been shot out by .22 rifles. As a matter of principle, professors never entered the hall. This placement was a deliberate act by a hostile professor of Greek who noticed Schaeffer was a 'pre-ministerial student'. His grey box against their shiny trunks, his clothes against their flannels and blazers, his working-class background and manners against their Southern aristocratic attitudes — at every point there was contrast and potential conflict. He was the 'Yankee', 'Philly' from Philadelphia. Schaeffer was in for some testing times.

His character was up to the test and so was his faith. A diary entry for December 1930 had read: 'May I always be in God's keeping especially in social functions', and 'Have found real joy of living in trying to serve God and others'. Freshmen had to suffer 'hazing', being beaten with a paddle or stick by a senior. 'Philly' was beaten regularly by his room-mate (who rejoiced in the name of Snerp) until one day the worm turned, and Yankee Schaeffer (five feet six inches in his stocking feet) turned on his tormentor and defeated him. 'You're the biggest little man I've ever seen, Philly', drawled the Passage 'top dog', who had been watching from a doorway.

A further test of physical strength as well as of character came as a result of Schaeffer's insistence on trying to start a prayer meeting in the hall. He would read a passage of Scripture, make a comment or two and ask if anyone wanted to pray; a few might pray and Schaeffer would close in prayer. His persistence in asking men to attend, however, caused one student to throw a can of talcum powder at him, cutting him above the eye. Undeterred, he asked again, and his assailant agreed on condition that Schaeffer carried him.

He was six feet two inches tall. Schaeffer did so, down the unlit stairs, to the meeting on the floor below.

A further example of his desire to do spiritual good was the help he gave to drunk students returning to halls on Saturday nights. Even during Prohibition the men could find too much to drink and on returning to Cushing Hall were not able to find their rooms. Schaeffer (who would be studying) agreed to come for them at the door, give them a cold shower and put them to bed. Payback time was Sunday morning. Schaeffer struck the bargain with them that, in return for his help on Saturdays, they had to come to church with him. Edith (in *The Tapestry*) makes the point that if anyone were to ask what Schaeffer's apologetics in college were, the reply should be that 'he had such a sense of the lostness of people that he did what he felt would help them to be shaken or startled to the point of listening when he would give them the truth in some manner'. That needs to be borne in mind in assessing his later ministry.

From January 1932 Schaeffer regularly visited a Sunday school for black children in a church called 'Mercy Seat', which met in a wooden shack through the woods not far from the college. For four years he rarely missed a Sunday, teaching eight to thirteen year olds. One girl, Martha, continued to correspond with him for many years. He also faithfully visited a black college cleaner, Johnny Morton, during a long illness and visited his grave at Mercy Seat when he died.

Was Schaeffer doing any work amidst all this? He certainly was, and doing very well. He was diligent as well as able (though remember he suffered from dyslexia — spelling was never his strong suit). He was a 'straight A' student. He deeply appreciated many of his teachers, and his basic theology was worked out in these years as he learned Greek, Bible and philosophy. Short poems and prayers in his diary at this time give an indication of his spiritual aspirations at twenty:

> Oh, God, not
> only for a time,
> but for eternity
> may I serve thee.

> O God, I thank Thee
> for thy loving kindness to one
> who has sinned grievously
> Against Thee. Amen.

> O God, I thank Thee, that You
> use me to win souls
> for Thee.
> O give me strength
> to speak the words
> Thou wouldst have me
> speak to them. Amen.

In 1980 the college made him an honorary member for his contributions to human knowledge.

A year after starting at Hampden-Sydney, Francis met Edith Seville when he was home in Pennsylvania on summer vacation. Edith had been born in China on 3 November 1914, the daughter of George and Jessie Seville, missionaries with the China Inland Mission (now Overseas Missionary Fellowship). They had been working in China but were now based in Germantown, where George edited the mission magazine, *China's Millions*. The ethos of CIM that Edith brought to their relationship was only one of incalculable contributions to their ministry in later years. The founder of CIM, Hudson Taylor, insisted on entering into the culture of the people with whom he was working — not only speaking Chinese, but dressing like them. The mission was also a 'faith mission' in that it never solicited funds. There are strong echoes of these and other features from Edith's missionary background in their later work at L'Abri.

That was still many years off. Their first meeting, however, was also on the mission field in Germantown. Edith had graduated from high school in June 1932, and on Sunday 26 June she attended the young people's meeting at First Presbyterian Church. She went because of a friend, hoping she might do good, rather than because she thought she would get any spiritual benefit. Edith had been brought up in a home very different from Schaeffer's and was already familiar with the work of conservative defenders of the faith such as J. Gresham Machen and Robert Dick Wilson.

The speaker at the youth meeting was a young man who had become a Unitarian, and his subject was 'How I know that Jesus is not the Son of God, and how I know that the Bible is *not* the Word of God'. Edith fumed inside, but when, afterwards, she jumped up to refute the speaker, she realized she had been beaten to it by a young man. He was saying that although he realized that those there may think his belief in the Bible as the Word of God were influenced by a Bible teacher at college whom they would call 'old-fashioned', he himself knew Jesus was the Son of God and his Saviour who had changed his life. Although he could not answer everything the speaker had said, he wanted them to know where he stood.

'Who is that?' whispered Edith to a friend; 'I didn't know there was a real believing Christian in this church...' 'That,' said her friend, 'is Fran Schaeffer, and his parents have been real mean to him because they don't want him to be a pastor.' Edith resolved to comfort 'the poor boy' but not before she had had her say at the meeting, quoting Robert Dick Wilson and Dr Machen. 'Who is that girl?' whispered Fran to his friend. They were introduced afterwards. When Fran asked her if he could walk her home, she said she had a date. 'Break it,' said he (not realizing it was only to go to her girlfriend's house). She did and they walked home. They had met, as Edith recounts, 'on the battlefield.'

Over the next three years, till June 1935, their relationship blossomed. To read their love letters in *The Tapestry* in these days of tweets, texts, e-things and i-stuff is an education. They had each met their intellectual and spiritual soul-mate and equal. Edith gave Fran Machen's *Christianity and Liberalism* to read. While he continued with his studies, Edith studied Home Economics at Beaver College, involving chemistry, microbiology and psychology as well as English, philosophy and ethics, leading to a BSc degree. She gave up the option of a fourth year to enable her to support Fran, but when one considers all she contributed to the life of L'Abri twenty years later, such a course, including also dressmaking, dietetics, art appreciation and interior decorating, certainly was, in her own words, 'an amazing preparation for both practical and creative development.'

Fran graduated BA *magna cum laude* in June 1935. His father was pleased — to him it meant Fran had worked harder than most students. He was also awarded the Algernon Sydney Sullivan Medallion for the outstanding Christian on the campus during his four years.

He was now ready to enter Westminster Theological Seminary. At this point, a word of explanation about the theological climate of those years is in order. In the early twentieth century, the 'fundamentals' of the Christian faith, including the inerrancy of Scripture, miracles, and the virgin birth and resurrection of Jesus, were under attack from what was called modernist or liberal theology. The historic Reformed theology had been proclaimed and defended by institutions such as Princeton Seminary, where Charles Hodge, B. B. Warfield and others had been champions of the faith for decades. In 1893 a scholar called Charles Briggs had been suspended by the Presbyterian Church for adopting a stance later called 'limited inerrancy', which allows for factual errors and inaccuracies in the Bible, falling short of, and consciously opposed to, the absolute inerrancy position of Princeton. The conservatives seemed to be holding the pass. Even as late as 1910 the Presbyterian Church adopted five principles as 'essential and necessary doctrines' for ordinands, including a clear statement of inerrancy. Between 1910 and 1915 twelve paperback volumes called *The Fundamentals* were published, written by scholars including Warfield and James Orr, defending the heart of historic, orthodox Christianity. Yet by the mid-nineteen-twenties, it was clear that the liberals were gaining the upper hand. Schaeffer was later to say that it was because they gained control of the seminaries and the bureaucratic machinery at the heart of the denominations. In 1922 Harry Emerson Fosdick, a leading liberal minister, preached his famous sermon, 'Shall the Fundamentalists Win?', revealing what the conservatives who fought back would now be called after the twelve volumes. In 1924 the *Auburn Affirmation*, a document from the liberal leadership of the Presbyterian Church, objected to the five principles of 1910.

In 1927 the General Assembly of the Presbyterian Church approved a reorganization of Princeton Seminary to allow for a theologically more inclusive approach. The Princeton theology that had been taught for more than a century no longer reigned supreme. This was too much for the able and gracious J. Gresham Machen, now the leading defender of the 'old Princeton' position, and with Oswald T. Allis, Cornelius Van Til, Robert Dick Wilson and twenty students, he left to found Westminster Seminary in Philadelphia in 1929.

The issue was far from ended. Machen and others with him were also concerned about foreign missions: they considered that the existing Presbyterian Board of Foreign Missions was not upholding the historic Christian faith. In 1933 they established a new Independent Board for Presbyterian Foreign Missions (the board that would send Schaeffer on a fact-finding tour of Europe in 1947). For his part in setting up this 'proscribed' body, in 1935 Machen was tried by the denomination, found guilty and in 1936, after his appeal failed, defrocked. Thus far had the tide turned since the suspending of Charles Briggs in 1893; in Machen's case there was not even any doctrinal point at issue.

Machen gave his energies to founding a new denomination that year, the Presbyterian Church of America, which was soon forced to change its name to the more humble Orthodox Presbyterian Church. His tireless struggles came to an end with his untimely death on 1 January 1937. Sad to relate, battles continued within the new denomination and the new seminary. In 1937 a group led by Carl McIntyre split from Westminster over two main issues: total abstinence, for they were convinced tee-totallers while Machen believed in freedom for Christians to drink in moderation; and their insistence on the view of Christ's return called pre-millenialism. This teaches that Christ will return suddenly and will reign on earth for a thousand years before the final judgement; and that, until he comes, things will steadily get worse on earth. The group also favoured the dispensationalist Schofield Bible, which Machen discouraged. They formed a new seminary (Faith Seminary in Wilmington, Delaware), with the Old Testament scholar Allan Macrae as president, and a new denomination, Bible Presbyterian Church. Schaeffer would be the first student to register at Faith and the first ordained minister of the Bible Presbyterian Church.

This, however, is to anticipate our story. Francis and Edith married on 26 July 1935. They went on what they had planned would be a nil-cost honeymoon in cheap overnight cabins with self-catering. At the end of it was a children's camp they would work at together for the rest of the summer on Lake Michigan. Not everything worked according to plan, and the early days of the marriage revealed some of the differences in temperament that would make their relationship 'real'. Francis had a hot temper and could get very depressed; Edith was a romantic and an idealist. On the way back from the camp, Edith had a minor collision with a car in Grand Rapids and was berated by Fran as 'an idiot incapable of driving anything'. She never drove again throughout their marriage.

Their first home together was a third-floor rear apartment in a slum area of Philadelphia, a brisk walk from Westminster Seminary. They made much of their own furniture. Fran studied into the early hours; Edith earned their living on a sewing machine. They discussed his course: theology, philosophy, Greek and Hebrew. Fran loved the teaching he received from men like Macrae and Van Til. Each week they would share in a 'thorough housecleaning' in which windows were washed, rugs shaken and everything polished.

The summer of 1936 was spent working at a young people's camp in New Hampshire. It was this summer, on hearing of the 'defrocking' of Machen, that Fran decided to resign from the Northern Presbyterian Church and place himself under the care of the new presbytery (of what was to be the Orthodox Presbyterian Church). Among their evening discussions that autumn were such things as: how could people stand for God's holiness and the purity of the doctrine of the church and yet not become harsh and unloving? Schaeffer's books in later years would insist on the simultaneous exhibition of love and holiness. In later years Schaeffer would be troubled by his anger at this point with men like Harold Ockenga, who maintained a conservative stance but did not yet want to leave the denomination.

Another troubling issue for the Schaeffers arose from their perception of the nature of the Calvinism they encountered at Westminster. They felt that Westminster was verging on hyper-Calvinism, that is, an overemphasis on the sovereignty of God to the extent that human free will and responsibility lose significance. Edith recounts wives' prayer meetings where she was discouraged from praying for small practical things as not 'fitting' for a sovereign God.

It may be that the Schaeffers were not entirely fair in their assessment of Westminster, but it is worthwhile looking briefly at this aspect of Schaeffer's theology. The relationship between God's sovereignty and human responsibility is something Schaeffer wrestled with theologically and emotionally. His great friend Hans Rookmaaker wrote in later years that in his first pastorate, Schaeffer worked himself very, very hard, to the point of exhaustion, because 'when he was talking to somebody, he felt he had to convince that person. If he was not able to do that, he felt it was his fault that the other person did not accept Christ.' One day, however, he found out he had been wrong and that, while he had to present the best argument, he also had to pray that God would make it effective. 'We acknowledge that it is first of all God's work rather than our work. Then the pressure is gone and because of that it is not so exhausting.'

Schaeffer steadfastly adhered to the Presbyterian confessional standard, the *Westminster Confession of Faith* (1646) and, at L'Abri, gave a lengthy series of doctrinal studies based on it. Two lectures are on 'God's Sovereignty and Man's Significance' — not, interestingly, 'Man's Responsibility', which would be more usual. Throughout his life Schaeffer was insistent on the significance of human beings and their decisions and actions. He repeatedly emphasized that history is real and human choice is real. In this he is in a fine Reformed tradition. In his essay 'Predestination' in *Evangelical Theology*, the Princeton theologian A. A. Hodge wrote:

So universally do all the real governing currents of modern thought outside of Christian theology run in the direction of universal determinism, rather than in that of the admission of the indeterminate, the contingent, the spontaneous and free, that many of us who are the staunchest Calvinists feel that the need of the hour is not to emphasize a foreordination, which no clear comprehensive thinker doubts, but to unite with our Arminian brethren in putting all emphasis and concentrating all attention on the vital fact of human freedom.

Hodge is also insistent, as is the *Confession*, that God's foreordination is in fact the only guarantee of human freedom.

By 'the real governing currents of modern thought', Hodge mainly had in mind Darwinian determinism, which was influencing scientific thought more widely. Marxism and Freudianism were to hasten the impulse toward determinism. Schaeffer's concerns, certainly in later years, were very similar. He felt the need to stress human significance and was very anxious that a proper Calvinistic insistence on God's sovereignty and foreordination of all things should not deteriorate into a mere philosophical determinism which destroyed human freedom. In some contexts he would actually avoid using the word 'predestination', which unbelievers may interpret as indicating fatalism, and would use other phrases to communicate the same general truth, such as 'God's rule over history' or 'God's calling of his sheep', though he would readily acknowledge the term if someone asked him.

In his studies on 'God's Sovereignty and Man's Significance', Schaeffer strongly emphasized God's providential control of all things, rooted in his infinity: 'There is no chance back of God'. He emphasized that the value of Romans 8:28 ('And we know that for those who love God all things work together for good...') and of prayer and of prophecy cannot be sustained if God is not totally sovereign. Schaeffer stressed predestination clearly. Salvation is grounded in God's election. He then insisted that man's significance is set in balance with this in Scripture like a 'delicately balanced mobile' with reference to such texts as John 6:39, 40, 44, 47, and comparing Romans 9 with Romans 10:9-13. Crucial for Schaeffer was that as God is undetermined, man made in his image is undetermined and capable of free choice. In *True Spirituality* he asserted that there was no 'prior conditioning' at the Fall (CW 3:305); man is capable of making an 'absolutely unconditioned choice' (or 'free first choice' as he says in *The God Who is There* [CW1:113]), and if this is not so, man is not the 'tremendous thing' the Bible says he is. Human choices and history have significance and are not just a game playing out decisions God has made beforehand.

Calvinism is not a philosophical theory. It is a theological statement to the effect that God has foreordained all that comes to pass, not that all events in history have a cause within history. How one reconciles this with human significance is a philosophical issue to the extent that Scripture is silent. Schaeffer was certainly insistent that man is not determined by anything in the material world, or psychologically, as behaviourists would claim. His statements about man being undetermined are to be read in this context; he was not claiming that man's decisions and actions are outside God's decrees. His lectures on the *Westminster Confession* make it clear that his belief in what he called God's 'total providence' was unyielding. Schaeffer was not interested in philosophical coherence where the Bible left things open; in this he was a true Calvinist. He was also a true Calvinist in his insistence on the significance of human beings and their choices, something he accurately saw to be under threat from the philosophical pressures of the twentieth century.

The tensions within Westminster came to a head, as mentioned above, in 1937. Debate at a synod centred on Christian freedom, with Westminster emphasizing liberty, and Schaeffer and others emphasizing that some behaviour was 'unsuitable' for Christians, such as drinking, smoking, theatre attendance and dancing (though Edith had been a secret rebel at high school, loving to go dancing, a love she retained all her life). Allied to this was the attachment to premillenialism and an uneasy (though not necessarily justified) feeling that such Christian priorities as evangelism and personal holiness were threatened by the Westminster perspectives. The result was the founding of Faith Seminary and the Bible Presbyterian Church. Schaeffer and a fellow student found accommodation for the new seminary, and leaving Westminster, he studied at Faith in Wilmington for one year.

On 18 June 1937, Priscilla, their first child, was born, and the pressures of all that was going on in seminary and denomination as well as being a new father told on Fran, sparking off more displays of impatience with Edith during and after the pregnancy. In the car one wet night, Priscilla produced 'a rush of what could have been mustard' around her 'diapers' and simultaneously a 'gush of recently swallowed food'. The next thing was a crash — Fran driving this time. Edith expected an explosion; instead he confessed, 'All right, Lord, I'm sorry; it's enough'. He found peace. It is not that he was never angry again, says Edith, but he felt the Lord had taught him a lesson he would remember.

In summer 1938, after nine months at Wilmington, Fran graduated and was ordained. Seven momentous years of college and early married life were over. He was called to Grove City, Pennsylvania, about fifty miles north of Pittsburgh.

3

THE YOUNG PASTOR

Covenant Presbyterian Church, Grove City, consisted of eighteen members. It had begun life in 1936 as a group which had broken off from the 'big liberal Presbyterian Church', meeting in the American Legion Hall. Home for the Schaeffers was a downstairs flat in a block next to this hall, consisting of a dining room, bedroom (which went to eleven-month-old Priscilla) and living room. Seating had to be arranged in the Legion Hall for the service. In a later interview, Edith remembered it as being 'not an idyllic time' and 'unromantic.'

From the beginning Fran wanted to reach children, and hot dog roasts worked well. He filled his 'Model A' with boys (twenty-one seems to have been the record) and taught them about creation and why we are where we are today. They affectionately called him 'Rev.'. It was not long before he and Edith asked the church to help with a summer Bible school and, despite anxieties, up to 100 came each day for two weeks. People familiar with children's work will not be surprised to know that there was no influx to Sunday School from the summer school.

Fran also revealed his pastoral gifts. Visiting a farmer, he would take a chair to sandpaper as they spoke, realizing that to do something together made conversation easier. His fathering skills were not as advanced; he once returned home and Edith asked: 'Where is Priscilla?' Fran had left her at someone's home. He eventually found her happily playing in a house he had visited.

As the church grew, a new building was needed. A nearby town was to be flooded to create a dam, and the church building there was dismantled and reconstructed in Grove City, Schaeffer taking an active part in the reconstruction. Only he and another elder had the head for heights to paint the steeple. Edith helped with the interior decoration and a picture of a ceiling piece she painted can be seen today on the church's web site. The same web site will tell you that the church began to thrive during Schaeffer's ministry. When he left after three years, there were 110 members and it still appears to be thriving.

One further element of the work in Grove City, after failure to make useful contact with local college students, was a high school 'Miracle Book Club', inspired by meeting the national founder, Mrs Eleanor McCluskey, at a conference. 'This was the beginning of our work with young people that later grew into L'Abri,' wrote Edith, 'even as the Bible School was our beginning work with children that was going to include our "Children for Christ" work later. Many seeds were planted in Grove City.'

A personal delight for the Schaeffers at this time was the salvation of 'Pop' Schaeffer. He had suffered a stroke, and as Fran visited, his father greeted him with the request: 'Boy, tell me about that Jesus of yours'. He listened to what Fran had to say and then trusted the Lord for salvation.

Susan was born on 28 May 1941. Soon after, Fran was invited to preach at Bible Presbyterian Church, Chester, Pennsylvania, and received an invitation to join Dr A. L. Lathem as assistant pastor. Francis quickly got involved with the 500-strong congregation, again helping to construct a new church building — God was wasting nothing from Fran's upbringing. He loved the working people, and they loved him and his preaching. On 7 December 1941, the Second World War hit America as Pearl Harbour was attacked by the Japanese. By autumn 1942 blackouts were imposed, and Fran had to drive around on very limited lights. It was during a blackout in June 1943 that 'Pop' died after another stroke, Fran and Edith reading Scripture and praying with him.

Fran's pastoral work included praying with anointing of oil according to James 5:13-18, seeing a little girl's supposedly incurable tongue disease cured and spending time twice a week with a boy who suffered from Down's syndrome, giving individual care, and teaching with the aid of coloured blocks. Summer Bible camps were regular features of their calendar.

During his time in Chester, Schaeffer exercised a formative role in the development of the new Bible Presbyterian denomination and began close ties with the American Council of Christian Churches (ACCC). This was formed in September 1941 to represent separated fundamentalists as an alternative to the Federal Council of Churches, which had strong links with the World Council of Churches (WCC). The separatist churches would have nothing to do with the liberal ecumenism of the WCC. The first elected president of the ACCC was Carl McIntyre. While at Grove City, Schaeffer had become moderator of the

Great Lakes Presbytery of the denomination and a member of the Home Mission Committee; he also served on the Board of Directors of the Summer Bible School Association. In 1942 he gave a paper on 'Our System of Doctrine' to the General Synod of the denomination. He defined their position as Protestant, supernaturalist, evangelical, particularist (as opposed to universalist) and premillenialist (even though this eschatological position was not formally part of their system). Their doctrinal position he stated to be that commonly known as 'Reformed'. He insisted that this must be separatism not only on paper, but in action. He had little time for theology that was not lived out in consistent obedience.

After his father's funeral, Schaeffer received a call to First Bible Presbyterian Church, St Louis, Missouri. They had been in Chester just under two years, and though they loved the people, Fran was uncomfortable about plans for further building which he thought were extravagant. In September 1943 the Schaeffers moved to Missouri. It was to be their home until 1948.

Edith loved the elegance of St Louis with its great park, art museum, the Kiel Auditorium for concerts, large stores, historic residential areas, universities and hospitals. The church building was in red brick with a high arched ceiling, dark wooden beams and stained glass windows. They lived for a time with a family until, on Christmas Eve, they moved into a three-storey house with thirteen rooms and a large basement. The congregation was large, and Fran was soon involved in a full schedule of meetings, preaching twice each Sunday and taking a Bible study on Wednesdays, as well as attending numerous administrative meetings. Sunday afternoons were often given over to a visit to the art museum, where Fran encouraged his daughters Priscilla and Susan (and later Debby, who was born on 3 May 1945) to sketch what they saw. Fran's own interest in art was deep and growing.

One of the most significant developments of the St Louis years was the formation of Children for Christ. The Schaeffers quickly got a children's work going, using their basement for gatherings of the friends of Priscilla and Susan. Edith taught this class, but they also began to teach other women to take Bible classes with children in their own homes. Soon there were twenty such classes. Edith reckoned that the preparation evenings with these women were the real beginning of what was to become Children for Christ. They called the programme 'Seven Points How', the seven principles of the work being:

1. The home Bible classes;
2. 'Released Time Classes' — to make use of the one hour a week Missouri and some other states allowed for children to be released from school for religious education;
3. A programme for 'open-air work' on beaches and in parks;
4. Empire Builder clubs — similar to Boy and Girl Scouts, but with added Christian teaching;
5. An annual summer Bible school;
6. A camping programme to follow the Bible school;
7. A large annual children's rally so that the children could see that many others shared their faith.

At the first such annual rally, seven hundred children were present, and, needless to say, it made the pages of the *St Louis Post Dispatch*. The work spread to other states and across the nation. Because of the Schaeffers' close association with the separatist American Council for Christian Churches, the work was only open to children from those churches, a fact Edith remembered with some unease in later years and which they were not entirely happy with at the time. It was the separatist principle, however, which led to the formal establishment of Children for Christ. Fran had been a prime mover in the local Child Evangelism Fellowship until the CEF Board told him to stop running it as a separatist organization. In 1945, at the meetings of the ACCC held in St Louis, Children for Christ was set up on a national basis, Fran being Director. It was a big part of their lives in St Louis, and it played a major part in their moving to Europe, as we shall see. They were involved in it until after L'Abri was established in 1955. The movement finally closed down in 1982; by then the Schaeffers were actively supporting an organization called Help a Child, Inc., operating in Africa and Asia, run by their good friend Anky Rookmaaker.

Fran was showing energy and vision as a pastor, but also making it clear he was prepared to challenge the culture of even a separatist church if need be. He had already shown unease over building plans in Chester; in St Louis he told the elders that he would resign if the church moved from the city to the suburbs, which was what more affluent citizens were doing in those days. He also warned them he would resign if a black person came to the church and was made to feel unwelcome. That sounds ordinary now; it was much less so in 1943.

In the month they moved to St Louis, September 1943, the first American troops were sent to fight in Europe, which was being torn apart by the Second World War. Fran would say to the young soldiers going out that while they were doing the right thing to fight, if there was hatred in their heart personally against the people they were fighting, it was wrong. This was something he would stress often in later years when asked for his views on war and pacifism. In late 1943 he also published a pamphlet addressing the issue of anti-Semitism, entitled 'The Bible-believing Christian and the Jew', which was distributed in the thousands.

As well as being active in the Bible Presbyterian denomination at home, Fran took great interest in the work of the Independent Board for Presbyterian Foreign Missions, set up by J. Gresham Machen in 1933, and soon was elected a board member. Overseas mission was never far from the minds of Fran and Edith. In seminary days they had a map of China on their kitchen wall; in St Louis they had an old mirror frame on their wall with black and white prints of scenes from Asia in it alongside the words 'Go ye into all the world...' In the spring of 1947, two years after the war in Europe ended, the board discussed the situation in Europe. Two things concerned Fran: the state of children's work, and the encroaching theological liberalism, especially the thinking of the neo-orthodox theologian Karl Barth. Fran suggested to the board that they should find out what the situation in Europe was. The board decided to send him. He was to go on a three-month fact-finding tour, leaving in July 1947. In addition to going as a member of the Independent Board, he bore the rather bureaucratic title of American Secretary, Foreign Relations Department, of the ACCC. Edith and the children would live at Brewster, Cape Cod, while another minister took over their house in St Louis to cover for Fran.

4

Europe, 1947

There was something of the frontiersman and pioneer about Schaeffer. Tough, wiry and practical, a century earlier he would have been seen more readily as a circuit preacher in the 'wild west' rather than settling down in some civilized east coast pastorate or academic institution. In later years he often said his favourite reformer was William Farel, the fiery, roving evangelist of the Swiss canton of Vaud where L'Abri was to begin in 1955.

From July to September 1947, Schaeffer experienced his own gruelling mission, travelling through thirteen European countries in ninety days, visiting thirty-one cities, staying in fifty-six different places and keeping 180 appointments, often with key Christian leaders, as well as speaking engagements. The Second World War had ended in 1945. Travelling was difficult, good food was scarce, and cities and towns bore the scars of bombing and fighting. His flight via Newfoundland and Ireland took him to Paris, and much of his first month was spent in France and Switzerland, travelling largely in crowded trains. He visited the Reformed

Seminary in Aix-en-Provence. In Geneva he was thrilled at
the Reformation heritage as he saw the site where Calvin
died and St Peter's Cathedral where Calvin and Knox had
preached. In Lausanne he spoke with theologian René
Pache. At Beatenberg, after 'the most beautiful' train ride
he had ever experienced, over the Alps, he met with the
director of Emmaus Bible Institute, Dr de Benoit, who knew
Karl Barth as a boy. 'He sees the need of separation clearly,'
wrote Schaeffer. He discovered a difference between France,
where there were Bible-believing churches, and Switzerland,
where Bible-believing Christians were only 'groups'. At
a conference at Beatenberg he met various pastors and
Christian leaders and spoke on the ACCC and the hope of
developing an International Council of Churches separate
from the World Council of Churches.

From Switzerland, via Paris, he flew to Oslo and the
Young People's Conference of the World Council of
Churches. He heard Dr Visser 't Hooft speak, urging the
young people to assume leadership and drive out the
'greyheads' who opposed the new World Council. He heard
Reinhold Niebuhr and concluded that he was 'the thinker for
this group'. Schaeffer realized that something theologically
significant was happening. The old style liberalism of Harry
Emerson Fosdick (of 'Shall the Fundamentalists Win?' fame)
was considered to be from the 'Dark Ages'. The real enemy
of the gospel now was the neo-orthodoxy of Barth, which
used biblical language and concepts whilst understanding
the Bible to be fallible. The Bible, it was said, could teach
spiritual truth while being inaccurate on historical and
scientific matters. Schaeffer would later call this 'semantic
mysticism' and fight it with all his might. Just now, however,
he was learning how potent and poisonous it was.

The effect of the World Council of Churches conference was to make him feel 'tired and lonely. The loneliness was more than personal. The whole Conference makes me desperately lonely for some Christian contact.' He was encouraged by a Sunday service in a Baptist church and then attended a Greek Orthodox communion laid on for the young people on the Monday morning. He was dismayed by the number of Protestant youth participating but 'far worse was the fact that even this was nearer my heart than what the Protestant men have been giving here' [that is, at the WCC sessions]. He did find great refreshment, however, in visiting the evangelical theologian Professor Ole Hallesby in his beautiful old farmhouse seventy-five pot-holed miles from Oslo. He was delighted to discover that Hallesby shared his concerns about Barth.

The following day Schaeffer was admitted to hospital with a temperature of 104° F and dosed with penicillin. He was delighted with the treatment he received in hospital; even his hotel sent him a bunch of flowers and a 'get well' card.

From Oslo he flew to Copenhagen and then visited Germany, where he was horrified by the bomb damage, and stood in the Nuremberg stadium where Hitler had only a few years earlier rallied his followers. He went on to visit Czechoslovakia (now the Czech Republic and Slovakia). This was just before the Soviet takeover of this land, and Edith writes, 'As an American Fran felt sick that the Americans had held back to let the Russians come in...' From there he visited Vienna in Austria, then Italy, where he was horrified by the war damage in Venice. He spent five days in Rome and visited Naples before going on to Athens (Greece), Holland and Belgium, with a brief return trip to Switzerland before ending his tour in England and Scotland. In Holland he met Professor Gerrit Berkouwer and in England Frank Houghton and Dr Martyn Lloyd-Jones.

Throughout Schaeffer's letters to Edith during this trip, there are plenty of 'touristy' snippets, yet much that would have significance for later years. He writes of hours spent sorting out travel documents in Geneva, then a rain-soaked walk along the river: 'Supper was the best meal I have had in Europe. Switzerland is much better off than France, and things are much cheaper.' We have already seen his thrill at the train ride through the Alps. From a cable car, 'The lights of the villages were like a thousand stars.' Arriving in Beatenberg, 'A boy pulled my suitcase in a wagon to the Bible School. I had supper of bread, cheese and marmalade.' He delighted in the sights of Venice, writes Edith, 'without tourists, without cafes on the cobblestones, without violinists.' He enjoyed the sights of Athens and Amsterdam, felt that England had 'a beauty that surpasses any other in Europe, except Switzerland, and maybe Holland', and explored the historical sites of London and Edinburgh.

'As you read the bits from the letters', writes Edith, 'you must add that in every city Fran squeezed in visits to art museums, historic sites or ruins, and other museums as well. This was when he became enthralled with the marvels of painting and sculpture as he saw the originals of the old masters. No one was walking around instructing him; no one had given him help ahead of time as to what to look for. It was a case of love at first sight. An appreciation for art was born.'

We may say that this is slightly overlooking the real appreciation of art that Fran already had, but in Europe the spark was fanned into flame.

Throughout Schaeffer's letters we also see a Christian bearing natural witness to his Lord. In Oslo he took an evening walk, ate a sandwich, met two Oxford men and talked to them of Christian things till 1.00 am. One was a Roman Catholic. 'I hope the Lord will bless my talk with them', he wrote. He was conscious of the Lord's oversight in all his practical arrangements: 'Our God is a God of details.' Perhaps the most strenuous test of faith came on the journey back. Flying over the Atlantic, both motors on his side of the plane stopped at once. The plane fell about 3000 feet; they were told to put on their lifebelts. Fran envisaged spending the night on an aeroplane wing in the ocean. His chief concern was his notebook, which was very heavy — he was glad he had lost so much weight that he could stuff it into his trousers. Meanwhile in St Louis (to which the family had now returned), a friend telephoned Edith to say he had picked up on his home radio an SOS from a plane falling over the Atlantic. Edith and the girls began to pray. Fran was praying. The engines started again. Fran arrived home safely. 'My Father in heaven started it because I was praying,' Fran later told the pilot, who was amazed that two engines on the same wing should both stop and then restart.

The purpose of the trip had been to study the situation in European churches and to seek out those Bible-believing Christians and churches who would be interested in a future International Council of like-minded churches. He had gone with practically no names or contacts; one had led to another. He wrote in his last letter on the train from New York to St Louis:

The trip is ended. This has been the great spiritual experience of my life, second only to my conversion. It has been wonderful to realize the unity of the church of Christ, and I have realised anew how right we have been in separating ourselves from the modern unbelief which is the new paganism. I have never felt more sure that our stand in the last twenty years has been the right one. Daily I have felt the Lord's hand upon my shoulder.

Fran learnt something else on this trip: the cost of serving the Lord. When he returned, he was in a state of mental and physical collapse. Three months of constant travelling, missed sleep, poor diet, two meetings a day for ninety days, public speaking, living in foreign cultures and out of a suitcase, had taken their toll. He also desperately missed the emotional and physical closeness of Edith. 'He needed long hours of sleep, his favourite food, fireside times of talking and reading together, and privacy with me,' she wrote. In due course he was able to take engagements to speak about the visit. He prepared a well-received report for the International Board for Presbyterian Foreign Missions and the ACCC, summing up his findings thus: 'To meet the basic need of Europe we need two things — missions, and an international Council of Bible-believing churches.'

The one thing of which he and Edith had as yet no idea was the life-changing significance of the European trip for their own lives and Fran's ministry.

5

BACK TO EUROPE, 1948

Fran and Edith settled back into their busy pastoral life in St Louis, but the resumed routine was not to last long. Letters began arriving from Europe both from people Fran had met and from others who had failed to see him but had questions to ask. Some letters were invitations to speak, some expressed the desire for fellowship. There were also many requests from within America to speak on his visit. The Independent (Mission) Board met and decided that Fran and Edith should be sent to Europe 'to help strengthen the things that remain' (see Revelation 3:2).

It is worth noting here that in going to Europe, Fran and Edith were not freelance volunteers, 'doing their own thing'. They were obeying a call from their denomination which, in return, was responding to requests from Europe. Of course, the Schaeffers became convinced that all this was God's will. This feature of Schaeffer's unusual life is worth emphasizing too in relation to the future founding of L'Abri. They did not set up a 'retreat' and invite young people to come to them. The people were already beginning to come, and came in ever greater numbers: the Schaeffers were then, as now in 1948, responding to a call they saw God evidently making on their lives. Were they willing to 'Go into all the world...' as the poster in their St Louis bedroom challenged them? Yes, they were.

The task set them after clarification with the Independent Board was twofold: first, in the short term to go to Amsterdam to set up meetings for the formation of the International Council of Christian Churches in August 1948. The broader task was to represent the Independent Board wherever the Lord would lead them in Europe. The General Secretary of the Independent Board expressed their thinking thus: Christianity in Europe was 'fighting for its very life against many foes' and among these foes 'the most subtle is that form of unbelief which in present day Protestantism has come to be known as modernism', which as 'Mr Schaeffer has shown ... is at heart nothing more than a cultured paganism as are [sic] also the system from which Protestantism separated long ago but with which modernism would now join hands in an "ecumenical movement" to embrace all Christians' (from the foreword to Schaeffer's booklet *Here We Stand*, Independent Board of Presbyterian Foreign Missions, 1948). Modernism (particularly the theology of Karl Barth) and Roman Catholicism were, therefore, seen to be the great enemies of the church in Europe.

Before setting off for Europe, Fran had to engage in an arduous six-month speaking tour of America. Edith and the girls went to live with Fran's mother — an arduous task in its own way too. It was a difficult time for Edith, facing what she admits was a 'dense fog' ahead, and also learning shorthand and typing to enable her to assist Fran. Two more little threads in what Edith vividly portrays as the 'tapestry' of their life were also stitched at this time. Priscilla was ill, and the doctor who eventually was able to diagnose her illness and operate on her (to remove her appendix) was C. Everett Koop, who many years later would collaborate with Fran on the pro-life film series *Whatever Happened to the Human Race* and would be appointed Surgeon-General of the United States under President Reagan. Second, Lausanne rather than Geneva was chosen as their ultimate destination on the grounds that, according to an official in the Swiss Embassy, it was 'really Swiss, and so much better for the children'. On such inconsequential moments, humanly speaking, hang much of our futures.

Eventually they set sail in the *Nieu Amsterdam*, arriving in Rotterdam in late July 1948, where they found cheap lodgings in Scheveningen. Edith's 'family letters' began on 5 August, the opening sentence being, 'It doesn't seem possible we have been here five nights already'. Food was still rationed. Edith encountered a cross-cultural challenge in the form of a 'Dominie' (Dutch Reformed minister) who smoked a cigar while walking miles to avoid using a tram on a Sunday. Fran, meanwhile, was busy helping to organize the conference to be held in Amsterdam from 12-19 August, symbolically just before the World Council of Churches was to be formally inaugurated in the same city at an assembly to begin on 22 August. Delegates from fifty-eight churches of various denominations from twenty-nine countries attended. The meetings were held in the *Kloosterkerk*, the church frequented by the Pilgrim Fathers who found shelter in the Netherlands before setting off for America in the early seventeenth century.

It was in this church that Fran met a man who was to be his closest friend over the years, Hans Rookmaaker. Calling in at the conference to escort home his fiancée, Anky, who was helping at the meetings, he was leaning on a wall, chewing his pipe, and began chatting to Fran. Hans, ten years younger than Schaeffer, was an art student studying for his doctorate. They talked about art, art history, philosophy of art and religion. They paced the streets of Amsterdam and sat in Hans' room till 4.00 am, Hans actually having forgotten to collect his fiancée! It was a remarkable meeting of minds and the beginning of a most fruitful and mutually influential friendship, ending only with Hans' untimely death in 1977.

The time came to leave Holland for Switzerland, travelling through Brussels and Paris with inevitable art gallery and museum visits, until they settled in their accommodation with Mme Turrian at La Rosiaz near Lausanne. She was kind, the place was clean, the views lovely, the garden spacious, but the rooms were tiny. Fran and Edith's room doubled as an office and bedroom; the girls' was a playroom by day and a bedroom by night. One bath a week in two inches of water was allowed. The boarding-house was also home to five elderly ladies and a student, so the girls had to be very quiet. Still, it was their first home in Switzerland. Fran worked hard following up contacts from the conference and his 1947 trip, Edith acting as secretary. The girls started at their various schools, and the whole family had to learn French. On Sundays Fran would hold a church service in their rooms. They prayed for others to join; soon an Irish lady from the boarding-house came and a divorcee from Boston with her two children whom they had met on the street. On Saturday nights the girls would run a 'young people's meeting'.

It was not long before the family paid a three-week return trip to Holland, where they stressed the importance of teaching children the truth away from the influence of the liberalism and Barthianism of the churches, and Edith spoke about how to use the home for children's meetings. One couple who did this was the Rookmaakers.

> 'If our work were to be categorised,' wrote Edith, 'it would have been labelled "Strengthening the Things That Remain". This was being accomplished through Fran's lectures on church history and just where the church is today and also through ... the International Council of Christian Churches. Another heading would be "Starting Children for Christ in Europe". Looking back now, we can see that there were no stiff outlines and that so much more was being done in laying a foundation for ourselves and others, for a future work, that only God could sort out what was happening!'

In order to recuperate after a bad attack of 'grippe' (flu), for July and August 1949 they rented a chalet ('Bon Accueil') in the Alpine village of Champéry, not far from Lausanne. The experience of living in their 'own home' led them to find another chalet ('des Frênes') in the same village into which, after a final two months with Mme Turrian in the early autumn, they moved in November. This chalet had much more space and room for guests, making Edith wonder even then 'if the Lord were not preparing to take us into a new stage of the work'. That first Christmas in Champéry, the Protestant pastor asked Fran to take a service for English-speaking skiers on holiday. The Protestant 'Temple' here was to play an important part in their lives for several years.

6

Developing Ideas

Pausing for a moment while the family is comfortable in Champéry, it is important to catch up with Schaeffer's thinking.

Apologetics

The first area is that of apologetics. This is the discipline of defending the Christian faith from intellectual attack, or commending it (giving 'a reason for the hope that is in you' — 1 Peter 3:15); or it may involve demonstrating where other religions or worldviews are defective. It is perhaps his apologetics for which Schaeffer became most well known in Christian circles. It is not so often appreciated that the framework of his thought was in place as early as 1948. In May of that year, an article by Schaeffer entitled 'A Review of a Review' appeared in *The Bible Today*. A review had been written by J. Oliver Buswell of a book called *An Introduction to Christian Apologetics* by E. J. Carnell. The book and the review were part of a debate about how to pursue Christian apologetics. Two schools of thought were (and still are) in debate. To put it simply: the older school, called evidentialism, believes in the use of traditional arguments such as those for the existence of God, the historical accuracy of the Bible, the resurrection of Jesus and so on. Presuppositionalism, on the other hand, closely associated with the name of Cornelius Van Til, one of Schaeffer's former teachers at Westminster, teaches that there is no common ground between the believer and the unbeliever because they start from different presuppositions about God. To use 'evidences', therefore, is to put the unbeliever in the false position of allowing him to adjudicate on God's truth. Reason is rather to draw on Scripture and teach from it until the unbeliever is convinced of the Christian 'presuppositions'.

In this debate Carnell was nearer the presuppositionalists (though not fully at one with Van Til), and Buswell was an evidentialist. Schaeffer begins his article by finding common ground. Both schools agree, he says, that the unregenerate man cannot be argued into heaven apart from the sovereign call of God. They also agree on the need for a convicting and regenerating work of the Holy Spirit for salvation and that there is value in talking to the unsaved man. Both schools say to the unbeliever, 'See where your position leads: now see where Christianity leads.' Dr Van Til, recalls Schaeffer, would seek to show the non-Christian that his worldview logically led back to irrationalism, and then show that the Christian system alone provides the 'universal' that gives an explanation of the universe.

Schaeffer then proceeds to offer what he calls his 'suggested answer to the problem'. The unsaved man is seldom consistent; if he were, he would be an atheist in religion and an irrationalist in philosophy. However, most are neither of these things because they are inconsistent. This inconsistency, thinks Schaeffer, is the result of God's common grace. Because the sun shines on the just and the unjust, most unbelievers simply accept life as it is even though their basic beliefs are at variance with it. Consequently, the average unsaved man has two parts to his worldview. First, insofar as he is logical (that is, consistent) in his unbelief, his 'system' is hopeless. This would include a complete scepticism (that is, uncertainty) about whether the atoms in his chair would not disappear or re-arrange themselves into something else. If logical, suicide would be the only answer (and later in life this was a point Schaeffer made with real seriousness and care as he realized just how genuine an issue it was for some of the people who came to him). Second, unless he has been totally logical, the unbeliever will also have what belongs only in the Christian system, but only by cheating, living in the world as if God existed and the Bible was true, but in his head denying that truth. 'Notice that those who cheat the least have least of that which belongs logically only to the Bible-believing Christian, those who cheat the most have the most.'

How may one reach the unbeliever? To the extent that the unbeliever is illogical we have a point of contact. (Schaeffer was later to call this the 'point of tension' and speak about exposing this as 'taking the roof off' so that the unbeliever is exposed to the inconsistency of his position and to the poverty of his non-Christian presuppositions.) This is where Schaeffer now shows himself to be flexible in his approach. He says that some unbelievers will need to hear of their sin and be 'brought down into the gutter.' Others will need a book such as Dr Machen's *The Virgin Birth* (a careful study of the evidence for the virgin birth of Christ). Yet others will need a philosophical approach, and so on. He does not deny in this, of course, that all will in the end need to come to the point of repentance and faith. Later he would say repeatedly that the sinner must bow twice to God: as Creator and as Redeemer; or 'metaphysically' and 'morally'. What Schaeffer is doing in this article is showing a pragmatic approach in apologetics, his overwhelming emphasis being on using whatever tools are at hand to expose each person's rebellion against God and his need of salvation, seeking to get him to the point of accepting Christ.

Schaeffer has variously been called a presuppositionalist, an inconsistent presuppositionalist, a compassionate presuppositionalist, an evidentialist and an evidentialist of ideas. It would be beyond the bounds of this book to discuss Schaeffer's apologetics in a more technical way, but it has been well argued that he is probably best categorized, if one wants to label him, as a 'verificationalist'. 'Presuppositions' in this approach are a set of basic beliefs which are more like hypotheses that can then be argued and tested. In *The God Who Is There* he insists on the importance of presuppositions, defining a presupposition as 'A belief or theory which is accepted before the next step in logic is developed. Such a prior postulate often consciously or unconsciously affects the way a person subsequently reasons.'

The relevance for the practice of apologetics is that although Christians and non-Christians have contradictory ultimate or metaphysical presuppositions, they share much common experience of life. Together with the operation of common grace, these provide common ground on the basis of which argument can proceed. Schaeffer was insistent too that what was shared was *common* ground, not *neutral* ground; that is, though the unbeliever shared experiences of life with the believer, he did so as God's creature and in God's world. Later Schaeffer would insist that the two things the unbeliever could never escape, and which always witnessed against him of the existence of God, were the reality of creation ('the universe and its form') and the 'mannishness of man.'

We shall return to Schaeffer's apologetics; but bear in mind that the basic framework was in place in 1948. An appendix to *The God Who is There* in the *Complete Works* develops, but hardly changes, his approach. The central principle is to press the unbeliever to the logical conclusion of his position, to find the *point of tension*, but the emphasis all the time is on using what is appropriate to the individual. Schaeffer was never interested in rigidly following a particular apologetic method, or worried about being consistent with a certain school, or being an academic apologist. 'When we have the opportunity to talk to the non-Christian, what (if not the formula mentality) should be the dominant consideration? I think this should be love... Thus, we meet the person where he or she is.' So if you are speaking to the Philippian jailer, you tell him to believe on the Lord Jesus Christ and be saved. If you are speaking to someone who has real intellectual questions, you take them seriously and try to answer them. Never was Schaeffer interested in developing or imposing a single apologetic system based on a prior philosophical position.

Love and holiness together

A second developing theme in Schaeffer's life at this time
was the danger of forgetting love in the pursuit of holiness.
He had become increasingly unhappy about what he
saw as a lack of love in the separatist movement, though
without ever, it should be said, doubting the rightness of
separation from doctrinal error and fighting for the purity
of the visible church. In February 1950 'The Balance of
the Simultaneous Exhibition of God's Holiness and Love'
appeared in *The Christian Beacon*. In it Schaeffer warned of
'the danger from within and the danger from without', the
latter being discouragement or compromise or withdrawal
from the field of battle. But the danger from within for
the separated movement was as great. 'We should say and
mean with David Brainerd, "Oh that my soul should never
offer any dead, cold service to my God!"' Soul-building, he
wrote, needs warm devotional material as well as scholarly
material. There was always the danger of losing love for one
another in the process of fighting a battle, developing a 'will
to win' rather than a 'will to be right'. The seeds of concern
about the quality of spiritual life within the 'Movement',
perhaps within his own spiritual life, and about the lack of
love between Christians who differed, are here beginning to
sprout. Very shortly they would issue in a major spiritual
crisis for Schaeffer, and five years later in his leaving the
organization that had sent him to Europe.

In mid 1951 Schaeffer wrote an article entitled 'The
Secret of Power and Enjoyment of the Lord', published
in two parts, for *The Sunday School Times*, which he said
'meant more to me than any article I have ever written'.
He expressed concern that in Bible-believing Christianity

there was not the consistent power there had been in times past and concluded with the words: 'When we have purity leading to love and love leading to purity, and all because we love the Lord — then there will be lasting power and enjoyment of the One who is the dear Lamb of God, slain for us, our Saviour and Lord.' Lane Dennis has said of this article that it 'set off a major controversy in the "separated movement" and marked a watershed in the thinking and lives of the Schaeffers'.

Barthianism

A third issue was his growing concern about Barthianism, or the 'New Modernism'. Karl Barth (1886–1968) was the major theological force among Protestants in the twentieth century. He had sprung to prominence after the First World War with a commentary on Romans which shook theological liberalism by the scruff of its neck and reasserted the importance of God's Word to which we must listen. He certainly brought Protestants back to the Bible and was, at first, welcomed by evangelicals. It became apparent, however, that his attitude toward the Bible was not that of historic evangelicalism. Barth was quite happy to countenance the idea of errors in Scripture as an inevitable consequence of its human authorship, but claimed that, nonetheless, God spoke truly through it. He even gloried in the paradox of God speaking truth through the errors in Scripture. Van Til at Westminster and others had severely criticized him since the 1930s. The division of truth into religious and spiritual truth on the one hand and historical and scientific truth on the other was intolerable to Schaeffer. Barthians taught that even if the latter kind of truth which was verifiable in the material world were absent, the Bible could still speak truth of the former variety. People could, therefore, turn to the Bible believing that God would speak through it to them even though they could not believe, for example, the historicity of the creation account or of the Fall. Schaeffer saw this as a kind of mysticism, which made the Bible simply a quarry for religious experiences divorced from truth in other areas of life; it was theology simply following the existentialism of secular philosophy.

Barth was Swiss and, from 1935 onwards, Professor of Theology at Basle in Switzerland. In August 1950 a Second Plenary Congress of the International Council of Christian Churches was held at Geneva, organized by Schaeffer. He took time during this conference, with four others including J. Oliver Buswell, to visit Barth in his summer cottage near Lake Zurich. According to Buswell's report, they discussed four central doctrines — the Trinity, time, truth and the infallibility of the Bible. The discussion confirmed for Schaeffer that, for Barth, there was a dichotomy between spiritual truth and the world of science and history. The way Schaeffer would later put it was that Barth's view took its stand like old liberalism on a flawed Scripture; logically he should either move on to pessimism about ever coming to know truth, or revert to the concept of the old, unified field of truth with a commitment to the truth of all of Scripture. The divided field of truth Barth adopted allowed him to have his cake — religious hope — and eat it: he did not have to defend the historicity of the Bible in the face of scientific onslaught. This, however, left Christianity without an adequate intellectual basis. It was 'semantic mysticism'.

The Christian and art

Fourthly, in March 1951 *The Bible Today* published an article by Schaeffer called 'The Christian and Modern Art'. His analysis of modern culture drew heavily on his study of art, from his early discussions at L'Abri in the later 1950s, through his books *The God Who is There* and *Escape from Reason*, to his film series and book *How Should We Then Live?* He wrote a short book entitled *Art and the Bible*. The seeds of these developments were there in the early 1950s. Early in the article he acknowledges the inspiration of Hans Rookmaaker. He makes it clear that he regards the artist as in some ways a prophet of a culture, expressing the essence of a culture, even as Rembrandt did for Protestantism. He drew parallels between art and theology, the New Modernism in theology (the existentialism of Barth) being the equivalent of Modern Art — both denying the Bible and its worldview and lacking a fixed reference point. The only difference he added was that 'the modern artist and the modern musician have been far more honest in portraying this unrelatedness'. A sympathy for and even affinity with the honest unbeliever as against the dishonest 'Christian' who hopes without adequate foundation, is here apparent. Schaeffer concludes the article:

> There are many people we can reach for Christ far better if we have an understanding of these things which exhibit the basic modern view-point, and therefore we can understand something of that by which today's men are bound, not only in spiritual darkness, but in intellectual and emotional darkness, which ultimately are rooted in and spring from that spiritual darkness.

7

TRUE SPIRITUALITY

In the preface to *True Spirituality* (published in 1971), Schaeffer wrote, referring to the period 1948–50, that

> *I felt a strong burden to stand for the historical Christian position, and for the purity of the visible Church. Gradually, however, a problem came to me — the problem of reality. This had two parts: first, it seemed to me that among many of those who held the orthodox position one saw little reality in the things that the Bible so clearly said should be the result of Christianity. Second, it gradually grew on me that my own reality was less than it had been in the early days after I had become a Christian. I realized that in honesty I had to go back and rethink my whole position.*

This period of rethinking came to a head in early 1951, though it had been building up for some years. The year 1950 had been a busy and not altogether easy year for the family, now living in Champéry. In March Fran and Edith made a lengthy trip to Scandinavia, primarily on behalf of Children for Christ. Later in the year they travelled to

France, where Fran talked to pastors of the importance of guarding against liberalism and Barthianism. After that, they went to Germany, where they visited Dachau, site of a Nazi concentration camp, liberated only five years previously. They also made contacts with U.S. servicemen in Germany. In November Fran went to Rome to observe the defining of the dogma of the Assumption of Mary (the belief that Mary was 'assumed' bodily into heaven); he was always clear-eyed about the deviations from the gospel in both traditional Roman Catholicism and in its modernist form as expressed in the Second Vatican Council (1962–65). During the year, Fran was ill during the German visit at Heidelberg; Debby was ill at Champéry; and Edith suffered a miscarriage.

Meanwhile, shades of things to come were developing. Near Champéry there was a 'finishing school' where wealthy parents from all over the world would send their daughters to learn etiquette and social graces, languages and skiing. Ages would vary from sixteen to the mid-twenties. From this school young ladies from diverse national and religious backgrounds started coming to the English services Schaeffer began taking in the Protestant 'Temple', following the invitation to take the Christmas service there in 1949. The Schaeffers invited them home one Sunday to Chalet des Frênes, and a weekly meeting began, to discuss their questions. Groups from other such schools came too. On one occasion a memorable evening in a local hotel saw Fran talking to a mixed company into the early hours on why he believed in God, making an impression on his hearers. A Children for Christ work began in the village. Edith, meanwhile, prepared teaching materials on Luke's Gospel which would one day be published as *Everyone Can Know*.

In early 1951 the family moved within Champéry from Chalet des Frênes to Chalet Bijou. It was at this time that the crisis growing within Schaeffer came to a head. He told Edith that for the sake of honesty he needed to go back to his agnosticism and think the whole matter through. He paced the hayloft at Chalet Bijou, still full of hay being stored for the peasant owners. When it was fine, he walked in the mountains. He prayed, and 'thought through what the Scriptures taught as well as reviewing my own reasons for being a Christian'. Edith was scared; she did not know where it would end. She likened it to a Slough of Despond (from *The Pilgrim's Progress*) and prayed. Many years later, Debby said her father's struggle was not really about what today we would call 'spirituality' (despite the title of the later book) but about basic questions such as 'Does this God exist?' and 'Is the Bible true?' She has also said that he really did mean that if he could not be satisfied with the truth of Christianity, he would throw it out. He was not just bluffing; and when he said that to people in later years, he was not just making a rhetorical point. If Christianity is not *true*, there is no point in believing it.

In the preface to *True Spirituality*, Schaeffer records that by the end of the struggle, which lasted about two months in this critical phase, he saw that there were totally sufficient reasons to know that the infinite-personal God does exist and that Christianity is true. He also said, with much significance, that he saw that as a younger Christian he had heard relatively little teaching about 'the meaning of the finished work of Christ for our present lives'. He concludes: 'Gradually the sun came out and the song came. Interestingly enough, although I had written no poetry for many years, in that time the poetry began to flow again — poetry of certainty, an affirmation of life, thanksgiving and praise'. Of this whole experience he said, 'This was and is the real basis of L'Abri'.

There were, firstly, consequences in Schaeffer's own life. His daughter Susan saw real changes in her father: '...the flaws in his character really started to be worked on from then on'. Little things were symptomatic of a change in attitude. He began to talk about doing the right thing, or a kind act, because it was right and not just as a 'witness'. Lane Dennis believes he emerged from the crisis with a new certainty about his faith, a new emphasis on sanctification and the work of the Holy Spirit, and a new direction in his life which would unfold over the next four years (*Letters*, p. 26). Jerram Barrs points to important consequences of the 1951 crisis for his later work. It gave him a solid foundation from which to engage in his evangelism in later years. Having gone through his own doubts and emerged strengthened, he was less likely to be shaken by listening to the doubts and questions of others. He also knew what they were going through and this gave him a tremendous sympathy for people searching for truth (or trying to run away from it), as well, of course, as insight into the answers they needed. Edith wrote,

> If he hadn't had the 'asbestos protection' of the honest answers to his own honest questions, he couldn't have coped with the blast of questions coming at him at times like a surge of heat from a steel furnace. He isn't giving things to other people that he has thought up as clever answers, in an academic way, for theoretical questions. He asked his own questions and discovered — and rediscovered — the answers in the Scriptures. A great deal of prayer is interspersed in his thinking — prayer asking for wisdom.

Finally, as indicated in the last sentence, he and Edith came out of it with renewed commitment to urgent prayer.

On one occasion he asked Edith, 'I wonder what would happen to most churches and Christian work if we awakened tomorrow, and everything concerning the reality and work of the Holy Spirit, and everything concerning prayer, were removed from the Bible... I wonder how much difference it would make?' They re-committed themselves to prayer, to a more real expression and exhibition in their own lives of daily dependence on the grace of God.

It cannot be emphasized enough that anyone wanting to understand Schaeffer should read *True Spirituality*. Most people become familiar with him through his apologetic and 'philosophical' writings, especially his 'trilogy' of *The God Who Is There*, *Escape From Reason* and *He Is There And He Is Not Silent*. If, however, he himself said that L'Abri would not have started without the experience behind *True Spirituality*, those books which encapsulate so much of his basic teaching at L'Abri need to be read in conjunction with this one. The addresses it contains were first worked out on 'scraps of paper in the pastor's basement' at a church in Dakota and delivered to a Bible camp in an old barn while the Schaeffers were on deputation in the States in 1953. They were entitled 'Sanctification I, II, III, IV, V'. 'The Lord gave something very special from these messages,' wrote Schaeffer in the preface to the book, 'and I'm still meeting those who as young people had their thinking and their lives changed there.' He preached the messages after L'Abri started in 1955, and they were given more developed form in Pennsylvania in 1963, then again in Huémoz (L'Abri's village base in Switzerland) in 1964. They were recorded at that time and, in that form, published in 1971.

What do they say? In the first section, 'Freedom Now from the Bonds of Sin', he begins with the imperative to love

God and our failure to do so, manifest most clearly in breaking the tenth commandment, against coveting; he takes us
through the work of Christ, living in the power of the Spirit,
in a supernatural universe, salvation being past, present and
future. The second section, 'Freedom from the Results of
the Bonds of Sin', examines freedom from conscience in the
thought life and what Schaeffer calls 'substantial' healing of
psychological problems and of the total person, of relationships and in the church. You will find that, time and again,
he comes back to 'the finished work of Christ'; and, in his
Letters, too, there is frequent counsel for troubled sinners to
have recourse to the finished work of Christ. It is clear that
this truth of living daily in the power of the shed blood of
Christ made a great impact on him during his struggles:

> I became a Christian once for all upon the basis of the
> finished work of Christ through faith; that is justification. The
> Christian life, sanctification, operates on the same basis, but
> moment by moment. There is the same base (Christ's work)
> and the same instrument (faith); the only difference is that
> one is once for all and the other is moment by moment... If
> we try to live the Christian life in our own strength we shall
> have sorrow, but if we live in this way, we will not only serve
> the Lord, but in place of sorrow he will be our song... The
> 'how' of the Christian life is the power of the crucified and
> risen Lord, through the agency of the Holy Spirit, by faith
> moment by moment [Schaeffer's emphasis throughout].

To get close to the heart of Schaeffer, read this book; his
sermons (in volume three of his *Complete Works*); and his
Letters (edited by Lane T. Dennis and selected from some
19,000 in existence from between 1948 and 1983).

8

LEADING UP TO L'ABRI

From mid-1951 the work of lecturing throughout Europe and promoting Children for Christ continued for two years. Franky was born on 3 August 1952. An American writer called Betty Carlson and a friend ('Miss Kansas 1950') visited and became Christians, Betty returning in later years to live at L'Abri. A leading Swiss resident of Champéry, M. Exhenry, was converted, with important ramifications for later years. The Schaeffers visited Spain and Portugal and witnessed the reality of traditional Roman Catholicism.

In March 1953 they left, via a visit to England, for missionary deputation ('furlough') in the States. They would be away until September 1954. In America they stayed in the tiny house of a widowed uncle of Fran's in Philadelphia. How that came about reveals an interesting side to Schaeffer. On the balcony at Bijou, where he had taken some of his agonizing walks in 1951, he had been asking the Lord where they should stay, and for one of only two times in his life, he said he heard an audible voice, 'as distinctly as I remember any voice I have ever heard'. Schaeffer was thoroughly rational, but no one who knew him would ever accuse him of being rationalistic because he never once doubted the power of God to act extraordinarily, though he never looked for it or gloried in it. After all, he believed that we do live in a supernatural universe.

Not that living in 'Uncle Harrison's house' was easy. It was not. God answers prayers, but it does not necessarily lead to an easy life. Fran, Edith and the four children squeezed into the tiny house, full of the things of Fran's uncle as well as their own. Fran lectured at Faith Theological Seminary (from which he had graduated in 1938) during the academic year 1953–1954 and was also often away speaking — in total some 346 times in 515 days. For one ten-week period in 1953, Edith and Debby travelled with him. In May 1954 an honorary degree of Doctor of Divinity was conferred on him by Highland College, Long Beach, California.

In July 1953 the first version of the *True Spirituality* talks was given in Dakota. It was when Schaeffer gave the seminary graduation address in July 1954 that it became clear that trouble was brewing. Objections came to such statements as 'There is no source of power for God's people — for preaching or teaching or anything else — except Christ himself. Apart from Christ anything which seems to be spiritual power is actually the power of the flesh.' Against the background of the politics of the 'separated movement', such sentiments sounded like a challenge. One wife of a denominational leader approached Edith after this address and warned: 'Edith, there's going to be a split in our denomination.' Schaeffer's message on the need for love alongside purity, for warmth, devotion and reality in spiritual life and for a real 'moment by moment' trusting in the Lord were seen by some to be an indirect pitch for the leadership of the movement. It was the 'McCarthy era' in the USA; reds were seen under every bed, and according to Schaeffer's daughter Susan, the leader of the separated movement, Carl McIntyre, at one time called Schaeffer a 'communist'. In fact the Bible Presbyterian Church did split in 1956 into two synods; McIntyre went with the smaller one, Oliver Buswell with the other larger and more open synod, which founded Covenant Seminary. In 1982, after various mergers, this synod became part of the Presbyterian Church in America (PCA).

The immediate effect of the tensions in 1954 was that the Missionary Board hesitated over sending the Schaeffers back to Switzerland. The family was appalled. They believed that that was where their home and work were, and they were determined to return. Would they have to raise their own support? So be it. The girls put up a 'support thermometer' on the kitchen wall and counted the money in. It was very low for months. They needed all the money in by 29 July 1954; the final amount came in on the last possible day. Such living by faith was to become a way of life for the Schaeffers in the years ahead.

The voyage back over the Atlantic, departing 2 September, was a trying one; Franky, just two, contracted polio, leading to permanent damage in one leg. Rather than take the train, Edith had to fly back from Paris to Switzerland for him to receive proper treatment. That autumn Susan (now thirteen) became ill with rheumatic fever. The local doctor who treated her was a Dr Otten, who became friendly with the family. He said he would like to know what Christianity was but did not have time to read the whole Bible. Fran thereupon produced a series of Bible studies (later published as *25 Basic Bible Studies*) which is still being used today. M. Exhenry, meanwhile, who had been converted before they went to the States in 1953, asked for baptism, and this was administered at a small service in the chalet. On Thanksgiving Day 1954 the International Church, Presbyterian, Reformed (now the International Presbyterian Church) was officially instituted.

Meanwhile, the storm clouds in their relationship with their denomination were darkening. The Missionary Board of the denomination expressed disapproval of Schaeffer's stance and reduced their monthly salary by $100. Edith encouraged Fran by reminding him of the name he had thought of for their chalet in Champéry: 'L'Abri', French for 'The Shelter'. Patterns of the future work emerged as diverse people came for discussion groups — 'a Cambridge physics professor, a Member of Parliament, a Spanish girl from Mexico City, and a Swiss hotel keeper's son from the Far East'.

Early in 1955 the whole village was threatened by avalanches caused by heavy rain and melting snows. Mud, stones and branches slithered down the mountain, sweeping everything in their path. The villagers, Fran joining them, dug ditches to carry the torrent away from houses while Edith and others served coffee to the Swiss soldiers who had come to help. The chapel had to be cleared of mud, stones and debris, but mercifully their chalet was spared. The full story is told in the first chapter of Edith's book, *L'Abri*.

Right after the soldiers left, Edith believed she was given by the Lord an especially comforting promise in her daily readings. It was Isaiah 2:2-3 (in the King James Version):

And it shall come to pass in the last days that the mountain of the LORD's house shall be established in the top of the mountains, and shall be exalted above the hills; and all nations shall flow unto it. And many people shall go and say,

Come ye, and let us go up to the mountain of the Lord, to the house of the God of Jacob; and he will teach us of his ways, and we will walk in his paths...

In the margin of her Bible she wrote 'L'Abri, January 1955'. On 14 February they received a phone call from the local police asking them to come in to discuss their permit. They felt sure that at last this was the five-year permit they had been waiting for. To their horror, instead, it was an order to leave Switzerland by 3 March — six weeks later. The reason? '...having had a religious influence in the village of Champéry'. Two documents, reinforcing each other, were handed to them, one from the canton (the local province in which Champéry was situated) of Valais, the other from the Federal government in Berne. There was no mistake.

Fran rallied the family. There were two courses open to them: either to telegram influential people and organizations, or to 'simply ask God to help us. We have been saying that we want to have a greater reality of the supernatural power of God in our lives and in our work. It seems to me we are being given an opportunity right now to demonstrate God's power. Do we believe our God is the God of Daniel?' They prayed for God's help. Prayer does not preclude action, and Edith felt it right to contact a Protestant friend, M. André, in Lausanne. His response was, 'This couldn't happen in Switzerland'. M. Exhenry told them the reason: the Roman Catholic bishop had objected to the influence they were having (particularly M. Exhenry's own conversion) and 'even a liberty-loving lawyer will fold up if enough pressure is brought to bear on him'.

They went to Lausanne to sign appeal papers. The appeal to stay in Champéry was refused, though in the

course of official contacts Fran discovered that the senior
American consul in Berne was an old school friend of his
from Philadelphia. To stay in Switzerland they would have
to prove that they had made financial arrangements to rent
or buy a house in a village, that the village wanted them to
stay, and the commune (local council) had to agree to this
and then apply to the canton for permission for them to stay,
after which the Federal government in Berne had to annul
the edict against them. Some might have wilted before this
bureaucratic mountain, but Fran and Edith started house-
hunting. Space forbids a detailed account of the events of
the following weeks which, as Colin Duriez says, read 'rather
like a new chapter of the book of Acts', but they were led to
Chalet les Mélèzes in the village of Huémoz in the Protestant
canton of Vaud. Financially there were three critical points.
First, they needed assurance that it was right to proceed.
They prayed for one thousand dollars to arrive 'before ten
o'clock tomorrow morning', and it arrived with a letter saying
that the American donors wanted it to help the Schaeffers
'to buy a house that would always be open to young people'.
The second critical point was the arrival of 8,000 francs
for the promissory payment; the third was the receipt of
the exact amount for the down-payment and completion
costs. After the purchase was finalized on 31 May, they had
three francs in hand. A remarkable providence had been the
discovery that a neighbour of the new chalet had a brother
who was one of the Swiss Federal Council of Seven, and his
intervention helped to secure the final permission for the
Schaeffers to stay in the canton of Vaud.

Four guests joined the Schaeffers for breakfast on the
balcony on 1 April, the day after they moved in (though the
full price was not paid till 31 May), but 'It was the weekend of

6-9 May 1955 that L'Abri was "born", writes Edith. Priscilla was starting university at Lausanne and brought a friend home because 'she has so many questions and is studying oriental religions; she needs Daddy to talk to'. Edith felt far from ready in the ill-equipped chalet, but Grace came that weekend and two other girls joined them for discussion, walks, Sunday services and Edith's hospitality. A way of life was being born. At the same time it was only a continuation of what had been growing for several years.

On 5 June Fran wrote to the Missionary Board with their resignations. The Board had indicated that it would not be acceptable for them to stay in Switzerland and receive people simply as guests to ask questions, and had made no further promises of support. It must not be thought that this decision was easy for the Schaeffers. Fran wrote to a friend that they would bear testimony that 'although the decisions we have made on principle have cost us everything into which we had put twenty years of interest and work, still he has given us a quietness of heart'. Schaeffer also felt strongly that they had both to give honest answers to honest questions and also a practical demonstration of God's existence by living by faith. They would call the new work 'L'Abri Fellowship'.

On 21 June their permit to remain in Switzerland arrived. 'After that first weekend,' wrote Edith, 'we *never* had a time without someone arriving on the doorstep with questions! L'Abri had begun.'

9

L'ABRI

In his preface to Edith's book, *L'Abri*, published in 1969, Fran wrote that the work of L'Abri,

has two inter-related aspects. First there is the attempt to give an honest answer to honest questions — intellectually and upon a careful exegetical base. My books, The God Who Is There, Escape From Reason *and* Death in The City *[the only books of his published at that time] are directed to this aspect. The second aspect is the demonstration that the Personal-Infinite God is really there in our generation. When twentieth century people come to L'Abri they are faced with these two aspects simultaneously, as the two sides of a single coin.*

Edith expanded on this second aspect in *L'Abri*:

We have established our purpose as this: 'To show forth by demonstration, in our life and work, the existence of God'. We have in other words decided to live on the basis of prayer

in several realms, so that we might demonstrate to any who
care to look the existence of God. We have set forth to live
by prayer in these four specific realms:

1. *We make our financial and material needs known to*
   God alone, in prayer, rather than sending out pleas for
   money. We believe that He can put it into the minds of
   the people of his choice the share they should have in our
   work.
2. *We pray that God will bring the people of His choice to*
   us, and keep all others away. There are no advertising
   leaflets [and L'Abri, in 1969, was the first book written
   about the work].
3. *We pray that God will plan the work, and unfold His plan*
   to us (guide us, lead us) day by day, rather than planning
   the future in some clever or efficient way in committee
   meetings.
4. *We pray that God will send the workers of His choice*
   to us, rather than pleading for workers in the usual
   channels.

These two sides to L'Abri need always to be borne in mind. It certainly was a place for people to come to find 'honest answers to honest questions', but that searching for the truth was always to be pursued in an atmosphere of practised faith and genuine love. Without this context, the 'honest answers' would not have had the impact they did. *Truth With Love* is the title of Bryan Follis's book on Schaeffer's apologetics, and it sums up the work well — people needed not only to find intellectual answers, but so far as possible to see, in 'faith working through love' (Galatians 5:6) at L'Abri, the reality of the God in whom they were invited to put their trust.

Where is L'Abri?

The village of Huémoz is situated on a mountainside on the twisty road from Aigle to Villars with a beautiful view over valleys and mountains. Chalet les Mélèzes, purchased by the Schaeffers in 1955, had three floors with twelve rooms and full length balconies extending along the upper floors. By the late 1960s several other chalets in Huémoz were either owned or rented by L'Abri Fellowship or by people associated with L'Abri. The letter I received when I wrote to L'Abri to arrange my visit in 1981 informed me as follows:

> *The community is made up of a small group of homes with their doors opened to those who have serious questions about Christianity. We do not have a reservation system so in practice this means that we try to be of help to each person who comes to us each day. Often in the summer our homes are full, so this means staying for a time in a nearby pension or farmhouse.*

In 1958 a flat in central London prepared the way for the first overseas branch, a house in Ealing (west London) in 1964, followed by The Manor House, Greatham, Hampshire, in 1971. There are now also branches in Rochester (Minnesota), Southborough (Massachusetts), Holland, Sweden, Canada, Korea, Germany, Australia and Brazil.

Who came to L'Abri?

Many of the earliest visitors were student friends of Priscilla (who began studying at Lausanne in April 1955, just two weeks after the move to Huémoz). Students followed from all over the world and from every discipline. Older people came — doctors, vicars, violinists, sculptors and engineers, some in their twenties, others in their sixties. Their background could be nominal Christian, agnostic, Hindu, Buddhist or atheist. I went in my mid-twenties in 1981, by which time, I was told, there had been a shift in the nature of people coming; in the 1950s and 1960s, it was predominantly non-Christians who went; by 1980 one was far more likely to meet confused or disenchanted young Christians.

Why did they go?

The visitors were serious in asking important questions. They would have heard of the place by word of mouth. No doubt, particularly as L'Abri became famous and Schaeffer's books well known, others went out of curiosity; some, for a cheap holiday in the Alps (though they would soon be disabused of that notion).

Typical of an early visitor was John Sandri, one of the first Lausanne students to visit Huémoz. Setting off on a walk with Schaeffer and Karl Woodson (an American soldier from Germany who, with his brother Hurvey, had been in the Schaeffers' children's work in St Louis) he remarked to Schaeffer, 'I don't think Christianity has a leg to stand on intellectually, do you, Mr Schaeffer?' As Schaeffer's answers unfolded over ensuing months, John came to faith and in later life remarked that what impressed him was the presentation of Christianity as a worldview that could measure up to other worldviews. He had found at the church he attended that Christianity was limited to a religious world on Sundays and seemed to have little relation to the rest of the week or the rest of life — certainly not to the philosophical questions he and his university friends were asking. He came to see that 'Christianity properly understood' was intellectually respectable. This, it should be emphasized, did not mean that Schaeffer taught that people should accept it simply because it was intellectually respectable, or that he reduced Christianity to a rationalistic system which could be accepted by the unhumbled mind; but he did attempt to show that 'properly understood' the faith of the Bible gave answers to questions in all of life that were actually better than those given by any other religion or philosophy. In a famous phrase, he would say that Christianity is 'True Truth' about everything, and indeed, if it is not true, there is no point in believing it. Remember that Schaeffer saw himself in a 'Paul in Athens' situation.

John married Priscilla in 1957, the wedding sermon being preached by Dr Martyn Lloyd-Jones of Westminster Chapel, London, who was visiting L'Abri at the time. Hurvey Woodson married Dorothy Jamison, one of the girls who had been at Huémoz that very first weekend in May 1955. The Woodsons became workers and headed up the work in Milan, Italy, which grew out of Bible studies Schaeffer took there in the early days of L'Abri.

Another record of an early convert shows that people responded as individuals. A Roman Catholic engineering student called Jose came with many questions and found them answered, but, he said, 'One thing remains before I can accept Christ as my personal Saviour. I cannot accept the Substitute until I really feel I am *guilty* and deserve the punishment He took.' He came to that conviction and found Christ.

What did they do?

From Schaeffer's point of view, the weekly schedule at L'Abri, developed by autumn 1956, looked like this:

Sunday: morning church service and discussion with tea in the afternoon;

Monday: evening Bible class for local people — translated into French, usually by Priscilla;

Tuesday: fortnightly Milan Bible class alternating with a Bible study in Champéry;

Wednesday: Children for Christ class in Chalet les Mélèzes for English-speaking children from a local school;

Thursday: Lausanne — café Bible class (mostly with students);

Friday: a 'weekend crowd' arrives, evening dinner and conversation;

Saturday: walks with conversation, evening hot dog roast by the fireplace (remember how the children's work in his pastorates started?) and family prayers and conversation.

From the students' point of view, the weekends would consist of times of asking questions and listening to Schaeffer's answers, conversations and walks. The centre of the weekend was the Saturday evening discussion. As L'Abri grew, students would come for weeks at a time to use the Farel House study centre (named after the sixteenth-century Reformer William Farel, who preached in the canton of Vaud), which began operation in 1959. The prompting for it came when three people asked if they could come to study at L'Abri: Ranald Macaulay (whom Schaeffer had met on his visit to Cambridge University in 1958, and who was to marry Susan Schaeffer), and Richard and Deirdre Ducker from the UK who were preparing to work with the Overseas Missionary Fellowship. Farel House soon housed a branch of the London-based Evangelical Library. In later years, students there were far more likely to be listening to tapes than reading books.

The structure for students that developed was to study for half a day and engage in practical work (gardening, maintenance of property, cleaning chalets, cutting wood) for the other half. The evenings would be given to discussions or lectures. Broadly, this pattern continues.

Crucial to Schaeffer's ministry was that he was a great listener. Dorothy Woodson remembered that 'When Mr Schaeffer would talk to you, there was nothing else in the world that was going on. He was totally focused on you and what you were talking about and was very involved, very interested... It could be from the most simple person to the most intellectual... He was really interested in people and it was very, very striking.' Maria Walford-Dellu was offered a home by the Schaeffers when her Roman Catholic family turned against her on her conversion. She describes how 'he had a way of looking into one's eyes for a few seconds, concentrating on you alone at that moment to the exclusion of all else'. In his discussions, she recalls, he would make them relevant for those present, according to their needs and the things they were studying. She wondered at the kind of life the Schaeffers were living, sharing their home with people on drugs or even the demon-possessed.

This attention to the individual was not just a trait of personality but the fruit of love. Schaeffer had a profound respect for each individual as made in the image of God. He was convinced of the rightness of Christianity, but this did not make him at all dismissive of unbelievers. He both respected them and what he could learn from them, and also realized that, in order to be an effective evangelist, one has to listen carefully, not just talk. One has to be able to answer people's real questions, not simply the questions one thinks they should be asking. Of course, he was always seeking to lead them to Christ and would make them ask the real questions if they were not doing so.

My visit to Huémoz in June 1981 while I was a trainee solicitor in Croydon was inspired by reading my second Schaeffer book, *The God Who Is There*. The stay was intended to be no more than a few days in a two-week hitch-hike around Switzerland. Travelling by train to Geneva, then to Aigle, I caught the bus up the winding road to Villars, and alighted at Huémoz. Chalet les Mélèzes was by then something of a central administration point; in 1973 the Schaeffers had gone to live in Chalet Chardonnet, towards Villars. I was directed to Chalet Bethany and to my bunk bed. I studied in Farel House in the mornings; the worker at Bethany (John Smith, who I recall had worked as a physicist for NASA) suggested some basic tapes on Schaeffer's thought. I have an exercise book of notes of thirty-five tapes and one or two books and lectures I listened to or read in the twelve days of my visit (I decided after two days that the rest of Switzerland could wait). They include tapes on guidance, the Bible, predestination, the Trinity, forgiveness, the biblical concept of law, Marxism and many other subjects.

Schaeffer was present and during my time there led an open discussion and gave a lecture on 'The Christian in Our Moment of History'. First he said that Christianity does not begin with 'accepting Christ as Saviour', but with the existence of the infinite-personal God. His being is the basis of all morals and epistemology (the science of how we know things). God's will is what brought all things into being (Revelation 4:11). Second, the Bible turns to morals. Not all things are alike to the God who exists. People are created in God's image. We were given responsibility; Adam and Eve used it badly. The world is now abnormal. Then Christ came. Why? As abnormalities come through moral rebellion, not metaphysical smallness, the incarnation is not the basic solution, though necessary to make the solution possible. The substitutionary propitiatory death of Christ is the only solution — the solution to my separation from God, within myself, from my body at death, from other people and from nature. Finally, history is going somewhere. We shall all be restored. Christianity, he concluded, is not romantic; it is realistic but there is hope. By contrast, an honest non-Christian must end in despair. The modern world has no answers within its own framework.

I summarize these notes here because they show, first, something of Schaeffer's style. It is a gospel message, but it begins at creation before coming very clearly to redemption and the cross. In a way it resembles the pattern of Paul's Areopagus speech in Acts 17. Second, it is phrased in vocabulary (familiar enough if you know his books) that is not typically evangelical or even biblical. The concepts are biblical, but language is used that will make contact with the kind of people he was used to speaking to. Third, it is significant to see that in 1981, when some critics of Schaeffer suggest he was absorbed by American politics and the abortion debate, he was still teaching a gospel message to ordinary students at L'Abri. At this time, too, he was struggling with cancer and was within three years of his death.

The highlight of my visit was a personal interview with Schaeffer. After a couple of days there, I asked if I could meet him and was told yes — telephone Chalet Chardonnet to arrange a time. To my abiding shame I was late — having tried to fit in a visit to Lausanne that morning. An assistant at the door gave me a slightly frosty reception as I grovelled, and I was shown to the balcony overlooking the beautiful valley where Schaeffer was seated on a reclining chair, a low table next to him. He warmly greeted me. I sat down. He was humble and charming. He had a pot of tea. He asked with a smile if we English liked milk in first or tea in first. I said, 'Milk, please.' He had already poured the tea. He began to pour it back. 'No, no,' I protested, 'it doesn't matter.' So he added milk. There were some shelled almonds in a little bowl. I ate a few. I talked about what I had learned in my time there. He mentioned Dr Lloyd-Jones (whom he called 'Martyn'), who had died that March. I spoke of my thoughts about becoming a minister. Where do I look for guidance? He was helpful but said something I remember well: 'No one can be the Holy Spirit for you.' He spoke of 'pietism' among evangelical leaders. I believe what he meant was that their view of spirituality did not adequately extend to the whole of life but was restricted to a narrow 'spiritual' or religious aspect.

What is life like at L'Abri?

Initially, the Schaeffer family had to do everything. This changed as people became involved, and John and Priscilla and the Woodsons became 'workers'. In 1961 Ranald Macaulay married Susan, and in 1964 Debby married

Udo Middelmann: both couples joined the work. Others, unrelated to the family, became 'workers' too. Some would become 'members' of L'Abri, the governing body of the Fellowship. Students who wanted to stay for longer could become 'helpers' and then workers if the opportunity arose.

The following extract from the web site of the English L'Abri should give a taste of what a prospective student would expect today:

It has sometimes been supposed that L'Abri is a place for intellectuals or intellectual pursuits only. This has never been the case. A wide variety of people come to stay with us, for many different reasons, from a variety of backgrounds, world-views, ages and occupations. Some do not see themselves as Christians, and come looking for a place where their questions will be taken seriously. Many people come to address living as Christians in the modern world. Every guest brings to L'Abri their own unique life, thoughts, interests and questions.

L'Abri is a place where we try to take all genuine questions seriously. Our foundational belief is that Christianity as found in the Bible is true. This means that a commitment to the God of the Bible is rational and that faith is never divorced from reason. Moreover, because Christianity is true, not only can it be discussed intellectually, it can also be passionately imagined and practically lived out as the Truth.

Furthermore, we believe that the life-affirming truth of Christianity speaks to all of human life and thought. This means our lives are not divided between 'sacred' and 'secular' activities, and that Christian faith integrates all of human life, including our minds, our hearts, our work, our play, and our relationships. This also means that art, history, philosophy, economics, psychology, education, politics, science, contemporary society, and all other realms of thought can be examined from a Biblical viewpoint.

One of the helpful things about being at L'Abri is that intellectual pursuits and discussion are mixed into the 'real daily life' of living with families and working at all kinds of practical tasks. This provides a place where people can begin to integrate their faith into all areas of life. This kind of integration is important in our increasingly compartmentalized world, and can be very freeing, but it may not be terribly glamorous. A 'Mountain top experience' is not our goal. You should not come expecting a secluded retreat environment. Instead we have tried to maintain the reality of life within a family setting. There are lots of mundane chores to be done, some perpetual disorganization and not enough space for visitors to have private rooms. You may find some of this difficult, but there is a reality to the environment that many have found helpful.

Some basic principles are set out on the L'Abri web site:

There have been perhaps four main emphases in the teaching of L'Abri.

First, that Christianity is objectively true and that the Bible is God's written word to mankind. This means that biblical Christianity can be rationally defended and honest questions are welcome.

Second, because Christianity is true it speaks to all of life and not to some narrowly religious sphere and much of the material produced by L'Abri has been aimed at helping develop a Christian perspective on the arts, politics and the social sciences etc.

> *Third, in the area of our relationship with God, true*
> *spirituality is seen in lives which by grace are free to be fully*
> *human rather than in trying to live on some higher spiritual*
> *plane or in some grey negative way.*
>
> *Fourth, the reality of the fall is taken seriously. Until*
> *Christ returns we and the world we live in will be affected by*
> *the disfigurement of sin. Although the place of the mind is*
> *emphasized, L'Abri is not a place for 'intellectuals only'.*

The emphasis is that L'Abri is not just a study centre, but a place where the students live for a time with the members and workers and, in that context, learn as much by daily life as by formal study. Nor, it should be understood, is L'Abri a church. People who say L'Abri is an ideal Christian community (and those who lived there would never say that, and the Schaeffers certainly did not) overlook the fact that Schaeffer believed firmly in, and wrote about, the local church. L'Abri was never to be an alternative to church.

Although it has often been labelled 'a place for intellectuals', L'Abri was and is open to people of all intellectual levels. Schaeffer certainly had a special ministry to people who asked serious questions. He recognized this and was glad of it, but he was at home with anyone. A *Time* magazine article of January 1960 entitled 'Mission to Intellectuals', although fair in its treatment, fixed this image firmly in people's minds. It said:

> *Each weekend the Schaeffers are overrun by a crowd of*
> *young men and women mostly from universities — painters,*
> *writers, actors, singers, dancers and beatniks — professing*
> *every shade of belief and disbelief. They are existentialists*
> *and Catholics, Protestants, Jews, and left-wing atheists.*

Schaeffer said in that article that,

> Protestantism has become bourgeois. It reaches middle-class
> people, but not the workers or the intellectuals. What we
> need is a presentation of the Bible's historical truth in such
> a way that it is acceptable to today's intellectuals. Now as
> before, the Bible can be acted upon, even in the intellectual
> morass of the 20th century.

In reaching intellectuals, Schaeffer is expressing a particular concern, but it was never an exclusive concern. His earlier ministry in Pennsylvania had been largely to the 'workers' whom he also mentions.

By 'acceptable' did Schaeffer mean making the Bible's message comfortable for intellectuals? He certainly strove to make it comprehensible to people who were very far from traditional Protestantism, and he communicated it in a way that such people could understand. Yet he never watered it down or failed to make clear that people could only become Christians by bowing to Christ as Saviour. In *The God Who Is There* he sets out four questions that must be answered affirmatively as the minimum content if a person can be said to believe on the Lord Jesus: (1) do you believe that God exists and that He is a personal God, and that Jesus Christ is God? (2) do you acknowledge that you are guilty in the presence of this God? (3) do you believe that Jesus Christ died in space and time, in history, on the cross, and that when He died, His substitutional work of bearing God's punishment against your sin was fully accomplished and complete? (4) on the basis of God's promises in his written communication to us, the Bible, do you cast yourself on this Christ as your personal Saviour — not trusting in anything

you yourself have ever done or ever will do? That some may
have been converted merely 'intellectually' at L'Abri is quite
possible (and there were, of course, 'converts' who fell away
after leaving); but Schaeffer, coming from the background
he did, would never be satisfied with that. Schaeffer always
delighted in people coming to faith; he and Edith used to play
the 'Hallelujah Chorus' on a record player when someone
came to Christ.

The temptation to idealize life at L'Abri should be
tempered by the facts. Early workers at Huémoz speak of the
realities of living there on a shoestring budget. The winter
months were *cold*. Wood for the stove was strictly rationed.
Picture Edith typing with a thermos bottle tied to her hands
to keep warm. Sometimes she would work right through the
night. Food was short. 'We ate a lot of cornflakes, and we
didn't have much, we really didn't,' recalls Hurvey Woodson.
The Schaeffers managed to have holidays in northern Italy;
a big treat would be a bottle of mineral water, and it would
be carefully rationed out by Fran. The work was also costly
materially and emotionally. In the first three years of L'Abri,
all their wedding presents were wiped out. They had people
with sexually transmitted diseases sleeping in their beds.
Drugs came into the house, people vomited in their rooms.
It was a costly work. Yet the Schaeffers were bound by the
consideration that it is by our love for one another that
people will know that we are Christ's disciples (John 13:35).

There were, almost inevitably, tensions in the home.
Space was at a premium and Schaeffer's study was always
his bedroom. Fran had a short fuse and neither grace nor
the years had eradicated his tendency to flare up. The
relationship between him and Edith was a remarkably close
and loving one, but a combination of his irascibility and her

irritating habits, such as repeatedly being late for buses, was a recipe for frayed tempers. Jerram Barrs, who was a worker at Huémoz and then with his wife Vicki and family at English L'Abri from 1971 to the late 1980s, speaks of living in a 'goldfish bowl'. The strains on family life were immense, probably too great. In the early days, the Schaeffers probably did not give themselves enough time for their family; this was realized and schedules for the workers in later years tried to protect their family life more carefully and avoid putting them under unrealistic pressures: some would say they never fully succeeded. We need to remember, however, that the Schaeffers were of a generation of Christian missionary who just gave and gave; it is the seed that dies, they would have said, that bears fruit (John 12:23-26).

Remember, finally, the importance of prayer in the founding and running of L'Abri. From its inception, Edith wrote regular prayer letters to a large 'Praying Family' — indeed she had been writing to family and friends since they came to Europe in 1948. They regarded this praying family as the engine room of L'Abri: two volumes of these letters covering the years 1948–1986 are in print, and these account for only one quarter of what Edith wrote. In addition to the praying family, it was customary to have special days of prayer, usually a Monday. Money to run L'Abri is largely by gift: it was Schaeffer's view that (unlike the church of Christ) any work of man can be stopped by God when it has ceased to be useful, and if no money was provided to keep L'Abri going, then it would simply end.

10

SCHAEFFER'S TEACHINGS

If anyone is familiar with Schaeffer today, it is likely to be through his better-known writings, which are inclined to be called 'philosophical': books like *Escape from Reason* and *The God Who Is There*. We shall come to those in due course, but it is important to realize that Schaeffer was by no means just an apologist, much less a professional or academic philosopher. All his work was done within the context of reaching people for Christ, and as his early life will have shown, he was a dedicated pastor and evangelist. His work at L'Abri was a continuation of that. The place to begin a survey of his teaching is, therefore, his theology, which as we have seen was very much rooted in the *Westminster Confession* and the Reformed faith he was taught at Westminster and Faith Seminaries. A good summary of it is his *25 Basic Bible Studies*, prepared in 1954 for Dr Otten in Champéry.

25 Basic Bible Studies

The God of the Bible is personal and triune (Father, Son and Holy Spirit). He is sovereign and he shows this in creation (he created all things out of nothing by his word and pronounced it all 'good') and his providence (that is, how he deals with the world now).

Man was made good, body and soul, and had a 'true, unprogrammed choice by which he could show his love for God by obedience'. He was given a simple test (not to eat of the tree of the knowledge of good and evil, Gen. 2:16-17) by which he could demonstrate his love for God, but failed. Since Adam and Eve fell, all people have sinned and are under the condemnation of God *now*.

God, however, has prepared a way back to himself. 'We can come to God through grace, because Christ worked for us. The finished work is His death upon the cross.' The first promise of the coming Saviour was in Genesis 3:15. As the Mediator, he is his people's prophet, priest and king. As priest, he offered the perfect sacrifice for his people's sins. Now exalted after his humiliation, he intercedes for them.

This salvation is personally received by faith in Christ 'plus nothing'. '...I urge you to consider Christ's invitation: "Whoever comes to me I will never drive away" (John 6:37). The *basis* is the finished, substitutionary *death of Christ*. The *instrument* by which we accept the free gift is faith.' On exercising faith, we are justified, God declaring that we are just in his sight because he has imputed to us the obedience of Christ. We are adopted by God the Father; we are identified and united with Christ as the branch with the vine, and the Holy Spirit indwells us. We enter a 'new brotherhood' of believers, and salvation can never be lost.

While justification deals with the past, sanctification deals with the present. Salvation should make a difference in our lives. Justification never changes; sanctification progresses till the day we die. Its basis is the finished work of Christ; the victory that overcomes the world is our faith. We must live out what we are in Christ. Bible study, prayer, witnessing and church attendance are central practices for Christian growth. At death the believer is glorified in soul, but glorification is not complete until the resurrection; the body is equally a part of God's good creation, which must be restored. Christ will return and rule over the earth for a thousand years (Schaeffer was always a 'premillenialist' in his view of the 'last things'), and after the final judgement unbelievers will be cast into eternal hell, and believers will inhabit the new creation.

All this, I am sure, given a 'tweak' here or there, particularly on the 'last things', will be standard theology for most evangelicals. Although he had his own way of putting things, largely determined by the people he was dealing with, Schaeffer's theology was orthodox and straightforward. The Bible studies are simply set out, turning the reader to Bible texts for every point Schaeffer makes, earthing the student in the Scriptures. There is no evidence that his theology changed in the remaining thirty or so years of his life.

For examples of biblical exposition by Schaeffer read *Genesis in Space and Time* (on Genesis 1-11); *Joshua and the Flow of Biblical History*; and *Death in the City*, drawing on Jeremiah and Romans.

Two Contents, Two Realities

The 1996 Crossway edition of the Bible studies has the essay of the above title bound in it. *Two Contents, Two Realities* was first given as a paper by Schaeffer at the International Congress on World Evangelization in Lausanne, Switzerland, in 1974. It well summarizes what Schaeffer believed were the priorities for the church in the modern age.

The first 'content' is 'Sound Doctrine'. Christianity is a body of truth, a system, and we must not be afraid of the word 'system'. We must hold the truth. There is a kind of 'evangelical existentialism' which divides faith from reason; one example of this is the advice, 'Don't question, just believe'. The acceptance of Christ as Saviour can be sadly abstracted from this system of truth so that it becomes little more than another 'trip'. Schaeffer records meeting young people who had 'accepted Christ as Saviour' in evangelical churches but were not even sure God existed. In addition, the truth must be lived out — insist on the truth of Scripture in public life, even if it is costly. How else will we be credible?

The second content is 'Honest Answers to Honest Questions'. Christianity is truth for every area of life, so we should be prepared to answer questions in every area of life — we should not pretend that the Bible gives all the answers, but it does give the important ones. This includes philosophical questions: Christians should not be afraid of philosophy, only of practising philosophy independently of the Bible, which is rationalism. Schaeffer refers to the three times Paul specifically addresses man without the Bible — in Lystra, on Mars Hill and in Romans 1 — and how in Athens and Ephesus Paul engaged in discussion and debate.

Schaeffer writes: 'Answering questions is hard work. Can you answer all the questions? No, but you must try. Begin to listen with compassion. Ask what this man's questions really are and try to answer. And if you don't know the answer, try to go some place or read and study to find the answer.'

He adds: 'Not everybody is called to answer the questions of the intellectual, but when you go down to the shipyard worker you have a similar task. My second pastorate was with shipyard workers, and I tell you they have the same questions as the university man. They just do not articulate them in the same way.' He is clear that answering questions is not salvation: salvation is bowing and accepting God as Creator and Christ as Saviour. 'I must bow twice to become a Christian. I must bow and acknowledge that I am not autonomous; I am a creature created by the Creator. And I must bow and acknowledge that I am a guilty sinner who needs the finished work of Christ for my salvation. And there must be the work of the Holy Spirit.' We must pray hard for the people to whom we are talking, he insists.

The final test of truth, he concludes in this section, is that you confess that Jesus Christ is God — Christian doctrine is the basis of faith and of fellowship.

The first 'reality' is 'True Spirituality', and predictably enough he speaks of what led to his own crisis in 1950–1951 and what he learned through that: the 'meaning of the work of Christ, the meaning of the blood of Christ, moment by moment in our lives after we are Christians — the moment by moment work of the Trinity in our lives...'

The second 'reality' is 'The Beauty of Human Relationships'. We are to treat all people as made in God's image: we are to love those who differ from us and who are even our enemies, even the enemies of truth. The beauty of love is particularly to be seen among Christians. There must be orthodoxy of community as well as orthodoxy of doctrine if we are to be credible. How else will men know we are his disciples? Two particular failures of the church, says Schaeffer, are in the areas of race and the compassionate use of accumulated wealth.

I have summarized these two works at some length because they say much about what was most precious to Schaeffer. They also go some way to answering those who have accused him of being rationalist (that is, exalting reason above revelation and undervaluing the supernatural) and of philosophizing Christianity.

The trilogy — Schaeffer's analysis of where we are today

The 'unifying theme' in Schaeffer's writings is, in his own words, 'the Lordship of Christ in the totality of life'. Schaeffer's best-known works are *Escape from Reason*, *The God Who Is There* and *He Is There And He Is Not Silent*, often called 'the trilogy'. (I shall refer to them respectively as *ER*, *TGWT* and *HTHNS*). The first two were published in 1968, the third in 1972. Schaeffer considered these to be his central works, from which the others extended like the spokes of a wheel from its hub, applying the Lordship of Christ to various areas such as the environment (*Pollution and the Death of Man*, 1970), art (*Art and the Bible*, 1973), culture, philosophy and history (*How Should We Then Live?*, 1976), ethics, law and 'life' issues (*Whatever Happened to the Human Race?*, 1979) and politics and civil disobedience (*A Christian Manifesto*, 1981).

It helps to bear in mind the times in which the trilogy was written. The 1960s was a period when challenges to 'the establishment' that had long been simmering boiled over. The key moment, in Schaeffer's opinion, was the unrest on the Berkeley campus of the University of California in 1964. First, there was drug-taking; nothing new in itself, but new in scale and in openness, and particularly because 'many students now approached drug-taking as an ideology, and some, as a religion' (*How Should We Then Live?*, 206). Under the influence of Aldous Huxley in a previous generation and the new 'gurus', such as psychologist Timothy Leary and poet Allen Ginsburg, young people believed this was the way to find meaning 'inside one's head'. The leaders seriously talked of introducing LSD into the drinking water of cities, not maliciously, but believing it would cure society's problems. At Berkeley, this hippie world of drugs was coupled with the Free Speech Movement, the claim for the right to express any political views; this became the Dirty Speech Movement when 'freedom was seen as shouting four-letter words into a mike' (*ibid.*, 208). Then came the New Left, the teaching of Marxist Herbert Marcuse and others. The old order was under attack: young people were looking for new ideals. Rock and pop musicians were the poets and prophets of the new age; but in the evangelical world, as his son later said, in the early sixties Schaeffer 'was probably the only fundamentalist who had even heard of Bob Dylan' (Frank Schaeffer, *Crazy for God*, Carroll & Graf, 2007, p.118).

Whether that was true or not, it certainly seemed that no one else in conservative evangelicalism was analysing Bob Dylan or the youth movement in the way Schaeffer was, or even thinking it worthwhile to try to understand it. Schaeffer did try to understand. He believed in listening, not only to the questions raised by individuals, but also to those raised by culture and society. There is a good case for saying he penetrated the turbulence of his times more than most. As was said of the men of Issachar, he was a man 'who had understanding of the times, to know what Israel ought to do' (1 Chronicles 12:32).

Schaeffer's analysis was that the young people were asking the right questions but coming up with the wrong answers. They were disillusioned with the values of their parents and the culture in which they had grown up. This culture was hanging on to 'Christian' values but had rejected the Christian basis from which these values arose. So, for example, the work ethic was extolled and practised, but the Christian evaluation of and motivation for work had long gone. Biblical morality was still the established pattern for life and law, but the older generation could no longer say why. Absolute truth had been jettisoned. In theology, liberal theology had taken away the ground under the feet of the church (and western culture) by destroying confidence in the Bible. The existentialist neo-orthodoxy of Karl Barth tried to solve the problem by urging people to believe in even an error-strewn Scripture; but as Schaeffer pointed out, Barth's theology was by this time only part of the problem, not its solution. The Berkeley students were doing exactly the same thing: having lost confidence in trying to find objective truth that would give meaning to the whole of life, they sought truth 'inside their heads' — or anywhere.

The story of how western culture became relativistic is the theme of Schaeffer's trilogy. One of the early tapes at L'Abri is entitled 'Our real enemy: Relativism'. This could almost be an overall title for the trilogy. How does he trace relativism's advance? Although the first book published was *ER* (from transcripts of taped lectures given in England at a Graduates' Fellowship conference organized by the Inter-Varsity Fellowship in 1967), Schaeffer had actually written *TGWT* beforehand; it is the fuller work and generally better read first. *ER*, Schaeffer said, 'works out [his thesis] in the philosophical area of nature and grace' (preface to *HTHNS*, CW, I, 275).

His argument is that the 'chasm between the generations' is due to a change in the concept of truth. In a former generation, people believed in absolutes — that certain things are true always, everywhere and for everyone. Moreover, they reasoned on the basis of antithesis (absolutes, of course, imply antithesis): that is, 'A is not non-A'; something cannot be true and false at the same time. By the 1960s it was apparent that the younger generation (and, it may be said, a lot of the older) did not think like that. The source of their thinking and this change, however, goes back a long way. Schaeffer takes it back to the theologian Thomas Aquinas (1225–1274). Aquinas accustomed us to thinking of reality in terms of two 'storeys' — an upper storey which we call 'Grace', which contains God, heaven, the unseen world, the soul, unity and universal truths; and the lower storey, 'Nature', which contains the created earth, earthly things, man's body and 'particulars'. One can picture a line between them so that one could present them like this:

GRACE

— — — — — — — —

NATURE

There is a line, but in a biblical worldview there is communication between the storeys. The line is permeable.

The upper storey, in fact, through revelation, explains and gives meaning to the lower.

Now, Aquinas taught the fallenness of man, but allowed for the intellect, or reason, to have some autonomy, or freedom from the blinding effects of sin. A consequence of this was that man, it was thought, could gain real understanding both of God and of life independently, without Scripture; in particular the 'lower storey' (the particulars of life) could be explained without revelation from the 'upper storey' that, in fact, gave it meaning. Men thought they could reason their way to truth. Philosophy was affected, then art and culture more generally. Gradually, in human thought, as Schaeffer put it, 'nature began to eat up grace'. The world of particulars, of created things, began to 'swallow up' the universals which gave them meaning — God, heaven and the unseen.

The effect of this was that man had no sure way of giving meaning to life, of finding some universal principle which bound together all the particulars. However, he continued to live *as if he believed in absolutes*, until, say, the turn of the twentieth century. By then, Schaeffer suggests, it is clear that people in the west were thinking in relativistic terms— that is, that absolute truth cannot be found. Beforehand, they were 'rationalistic optimists' with no firm basis for absolutes but holding on to them, their feet firmly planted in mid-air. They also held on to the idea of a unified field of knowledge, that is, that we could, by reason, discover truth about all things. This is typically known as 'Enlightenment optimism'. By the turn of the twentieth century, however, it was becoming clear that such a hope was futile. The note of despair was sounded in poets and philosophy and art. The Existentialists of the early and mid-twentieth century were the most logical and perhaps the most honest exponents of the philosophy of despair: truth cannot be found; the logical step is suicide.

Schaeffer calls the line between (i) romantically clinging to the hope of a unified field of knowledge and (ii) recognizing the futility of such hope 'the line of despair'. To move from the former hope to the latter recognition is to step below the line of despair. Remember, this is a change in attitude to truth more than a moment in history; and a statement about general culture rather than every individual in the culture. In *TGWT* and *ER* Schaeffer traces this step through philosophy, art, music, general culture and theology. The keynote is a slide towards irrationality in all the disciplines as people tried to find some meaning without any reasonable base. He notes with some irony that theologians think they are doing something new when they adopt a novel stance (such as in existentialist or neo-orthodox theology); but in fact they are only doing what the secular culture has been doing for generations.

What happens, of course, is that very few relativists have the courage to go where the logic of their positions takes them. They may admit that reason cannot attain to truth. They are living in what Schaeffer calls the 'lower storey' of life, but they cannot live without something in the 'upper storey' of meaning and value. They need a universal to give meaning to the particulars — or to go back to the beginning, grace or its equivalent, to give meaning to nature. This is what the Berkeley students were seeking. They saw their parents' bankrupt pursuit of personal peace and affluence whilst asserting religious and moral values that had no basis in any true faith and could not be justified by reason. Schaeffer had great sympathy with the rebels of the 1960s (more so than with the conformists of the 1970s). They were asking the right questions; their problem was that they could not come up with the right answers because they had no more access to truth or universals than their parents had. What Schaeffer rightly points out, of course, is that whatever people put in the 'upper storey', whether it is drugs or absolute freedom (licence, in effect), or sex, or some mystical religious experience, or an existential 'final' experience — what they are searching for is something that gives unity and purpose to life.

Schaeffer traces this theme through the first two books of the trilogy. He shows how the philosophers Jean-Jacques Rousseau (1712–1778), Immanuel Kant (1724–1804), Georg Hegel (1770–1831) and Søren Kierkegaard (1813–1855) contributed in different ways to the move below the line of despair. Of particular importance are Hegel, who introduced the concept that truth is developing — it is not a matter of antithesis (that what is true cannot also be false), but of 'synthesis' — the fruit resulting from the meeting of thesis and antithesis; and Kierkegaard, who spoke of a 'leap of faith' even against reason. Over the centuries the line between 'Grace', or whatever now substituted for it in the universal realm, and 'Nature' had become utterly impermeable.

In both books Schaeffer also points out the answer. The Reformation of the sixteenth century recovered the Bible as truth in all areas of life; and, within the Christian concept of a personal-infinite God who is there and his Word which we can trust, there is real hope of a unified field of knowledge, real hope for unifying the particulars of life, and a real basis for morality. We need to return to Scripture.

In the third book (*HTHNS*), Schaeffer deals with the crucial subject of how we know things and how we know we know (epistemology). He shows that the Christian basis has the answer in this as well as in the fields of metaphysics (existence — is there anything there or not?) and morals (how we know how to live and why not all things are the same to God). He insists that in all three areas — metaphysics, morals and epistemology — Scripture gives us good answers.

An important feature of Schaeffer's teaching is his insistence on an historic (or 'space-time' as he put it) Fall of humanity in Eden. This explains why the world is the mess it is today as well as being a place of unutterable beauty and wonder. Schaeffer insisted on human guilt for sin, but he also saw men and women as victims of the awfulness of sin. He often referred to the weeping of Jesus at Lazarus' tomb to express God's anger and sorrow at the plight of sinners. In his dealings with young people, Schaeffer saw many lives wrecked by moral relativism, and he often wept with them. He also knew, of course, that like Jesus at the tomb, God was not helpless.

There has been much discussion about the validity of Schaeffer's analysis. Scholars both friendly and unsympathetic have questioned aspects of his thesis. Ronald Nash, for example, a sympathetic scholar, suggests Schaeffer may have been better to treat the leading figures he mentions as 'illustrations or key figures who are representative of more general trends in culture' than as the sole cause or source of the ideas and developments he attributes to them. Others have suggested he may have been better to take his argument back to the enthronement of reason in the Enlightenment of the seventeenth and eighteenth centuries rather than to Aquinas and the Middle Ages. His accounts of Aquinas and Kiekegaard have come under particular fire, though qualifications Schaeffer makes to his arguments are not always given fair attention.

His work, however, has not been demolished, and in the big picture, it remains very persuasive. One thing we cannot help noticing today is the way in which Schaeffer, in his exposure of the triumph of relativism, identifies the essence of postmodernism long before that word came into vogue or the concept was being discussed. Postmodernism is rationalism taken to its logical and destructive conclusion. Realizing that reason cannot provide what Enlightenment 'modernism' promised, postmodernism took the line of exalting irrationality; so that even madness is seen as the ultimate form of freedom as Michel Foucault (to whom Schaeffer refers in *Escape from Reason*) argued. Objective truth has altogether been lost, so subjectivity is the only source of truth. Put simply, 'what's true for you need not be true for me'; and this is where the vast majority of western people are today in terms of religion, spiritual matters, values and morals. What Schaeffer demonstrated is that when reason is exalted above revelation, we are ultimately headed for despair; there is no hope of finding 'total truth'.

Two things need to be remembered about Schaeffer. First, he was interested in the 'big' picture and in this, as has been indicated, his case is well supported. Second, he was never interested in being a philosopher as such, and all his undoubted learning was never 'professional' in the manner of an academic, which is partly why some of them were very critical of him, especially those who did not share his utter confidence in an infallible Bible. The fact that he was not a professional scholar would not excuse slipshod scholarship if he were truly guilty of that. It does, however, mean that we should understand his work with reference to his purpose. I have found that if you read his books as if they were sermons, it helps to enter into the spirit of them.

Schaeffer's attitude is well expressed in a letter of 1972 to Colin Duriez:

I increasingly realize that really I have very little interest in theoretical apologetics at all ... because to me apologetics only ha[s] value in so far as it [is] related to evangelism... In this same direction I have no interest ever in writing another book on philosophy after He Is There And He Is Not Silent. *I might write short things but the reason I do not expect to write another book after the trilogy ... is because from this point on it would become more abstract apologetic and abstract philosophy and while I believe others may be called to this I am quite sure it is not my calling from the Lord.*

11

SCHAEFFER'S

APOLOGETICS

We looked at the early origins of Schaeffer's apologetics in chapter 6, discussing his 1948 article *A Review of a Review*. The other important writing from him on his apologetics is Appendix A to the *Complete Works* (vol. I) edition of *The God Who Is There*.

He first makes the point of the importance of flexibility, not formula, in apologetics: 'I do not believe there is any one form of apologetics that meets the need of all people, any more than I think there is one form of evangelism that meets the needs of all people. It is to be shaped on the basis of love for the person as a person.' Second, he insists that all kinds of people have intellectual questions even though 'blue collar' workers may not articulate them; or when they do, they use very different language from 'intellectuals'. These questions are often serious, and they deserve to be treated with all seriousness. Think of the teenager who goes off to sleep with her boyfriend, not seeing why it is wrong, or even being able to think in categories of right and wrong, while her parents may feel it is wrong but do not know how to respond as they have no firm moral base from which to work. The girl is probably below the line of despair (she has given up all belief in absolutes). The parents are hovering on it, perhaps about to capitulate to outright relativism. After all, what is to stop them?

Third, he talks about the 'Christian system'. His conviction is that Christianity is true; indeed, elsewhere he often calls it 'true Truth' to distinguish it from the 'true for me but not for you' kind of 'truth' of the relativist. Moreover, he insists there are good and sufficient reasons to know why Christianity is true, to the extent that we are guilty and disobedient if we do not believe it. Christianity is a 'whole system of truth' that gives answers to all the basic questions that face us as we face the reality of existence. There are two key aspects to this reality to which God 'shuts us up': the fact that the universe truly exists and has a form, and the 'mannishness of man', meaning that man is unique. These two great aspects of reality have to be explained.

The unbeliever is, therefore, a creature of God, made in God's image, living in God's world but living against the revelation of God in the universe and in him/herself: unbelievers are 'denying the revelation of God in *who* they themselves are'. They have religious impulses and 'moral motions' but have no explanation for them and do not know how to direct them aright. There is a tension between living in God's world and rebelling against it. 'So, the wiser they are, the more honest they are, the more they feel that tension and that is their present damnation'.

These people are lost evangelically (in terms of being guilty sinners but not realizing it or not even believing in objective guilt any more), but also, says Schaeffer, today there is a second sense of being lost, in that people have no meaning, purpose or morals, no final answers for anything. This is a result of having fallen below the line of despair. This second form of 'lostness', he says, is answered by the existence of a Creator. 'So Christianity does not begin with "accept Christ as Saviour". Christianity begins with "In the beginning God created the heavens (the total [*sic*] of the cosmos) and the earth."'

When Schaeffer speaks of two forms of 'lostness', he is not suggesting that they may be radically separated. It is his way of describing the literal hopelessness of people who have nowhere to look for answers outside themselves. It is much more necessary for Christians in these circumstances to be teaching about God the Creator. However, 'accept Christ as Saviour' is essential to becoming a Christian and is the answer to 'evangelical' lostness.

Schaeffer goes on to discuss faith. Faith is essential to becoming a Christian: not faith of the 'leap in the dark' variety, but faith that believes for good and sufficient reasons. Christianity, he says, is in one way the easiest of religions, as Christ has fulfilled all the conditions of salvation for us and we simply have to accept him and his work on our behalf. On the other hand, Christianity is the hardest of religions because we have to deny our autonomy, the very thing we are most reluctant to do.

Finally, Schaeffer answers criticisms that he is a 'rationalist'. He defines *rationalism* as belief that one can come to final answers regarding truth, ethics and reality beginning from oneself and one's reason, with no information from any other source. *Rationality*, on the other hand, is the valid exercise of reason and thought. He reasserts his insistence that we have no final answers outside the Bible in philosophy, theology or science. A man who submits to the revelation in Scripture is not a rationalist, but he has a duty to use his reason to understand and teach the Bible and to understand all of reality in the light of the Bible. The apologist must explain the Bible and man's condition to people's minds, but this is not rationalism — it is respecting human rationality. For this reason he was always insistent on the importance of 'propositional' truth — truth communicated in words that mean something. At the same time as he speaks, says Schaeffer, he is praying for his audience, recognizing the necessity of the Holy Spirit to work in their minds as they listen to his words.

One of his favourite illustrations is the 'torn page'. We are like people who find a torn book with only one inch of each page of print left. However, in the attic we find the other torn pages and, putting them all together, we can make sense of the book. So the universe is the remains of the torn book we can see; the Scriptures are the pages found in the attic. As Schaeffer says, we use our reason to put the two parts of the book together: we can see from the original remnants we have (the universe as it is) that the pages found in the attic fit, and that the whole makes sense. Then, as he says, the 'whole personality' can enjoy the complete story. To borrow the words of the Reformed theologian Herman Bavinck, this is 'our reasonable faith', but not a rationalistic one.

Another illustration Schaeffer uses is of the 'two chairs'. It is found in *Death in the City*. Two men sit in a locked room with nothing in it but two chairs. The room represents the whole universe. Each is sitting on a chair. One man, sitting on the 'materialist' chair says he will explore the universe, so spends many years doing so and brings his results to the other man. This second man looks at all the results and applauds the knowledge it has uncovered. But, he says to the first man, it is totally incomplete. Sitting on the other chair, he is one who recognizes the 'supernatural'. He has a Bible and tells the first man that the materialist view of the universe is utterly inadequate. Only the Bible can tell us the origin of all things and give an adequate explanation of all things in nature and history. Now although the two parts 'fit together' (the materialist's findings in science etc. are valid in themselves), only the 'supernatural' chair can give real final answers. So the two chairs are mutually exclusive as far as a 'worldview' is concerned. If we once suggest the materialist view is valid, we have reduced the supernatural to a crutch: 'as far as the comprehensive view of the universe is concerned, there can be no synthesis.' He then gives the account of the flight back from Europe when the plane engines failed. Afterwards, the pilot told him that he could not understand how the two engines both failed together and, more amazingly, restarted together. 'I can explain it,' said Schaeffer. 'My Father in heaven started it because I was praying.' The pilot looked bemused. 'I am sure he was the man sitting in the materialist's chair,' adds Schaeffer.

What Schaeffer is doing, of course, is to say that we can 'test' the validity of the answers the Bible gives. The 'proof' of a theory, he writes, consists of it being firstly non-contradictory and, secondly, that we can live consistently with it. Does the Bible give such a theory about the form of the universe and the mannishness of man? Yes, it does, better than any other. It makes sense of the 'two storeys' of the universe. Schaeffer is not suggesting that the only reason we are convinced of the truth of Scripture is because it 'works', nor is he denying the 'inner witness of the Holy Spirit' to the truth of Scripture; but he is saying that in apologetics we have good arguments for showing that the Bible is true. Moreover, if it was not true to what exists, there would be good grounds to doubt its value.

Schaeffer concludes this appendix with an anecdote about an older black pastor in Detroit who, after Schaeffer had spoken one day, said to him, 'thank you', not 'for helping me to be a better evangelist', but 'for helping me to worship God better'. 'I will never forget him because he was a man who really understood,' writes Schaeffer.

What is the framework of Schaeffer's apologetics? First, he begins with the doctrine of Creation. By starting here he embraces all reality including the form of the universe and the mannishness of man, the supernatural and the natural. How, he asks repeatedly, could personality come from an impersonal beginning plus time plus chance? There has to be a personal (and indeed Trinitarian-personal) beginning to explain all that we know. He insists that, ultimately, the options for where everything has come from are very few — absolutely nothing, or an impersonal beginning, or an eternal dualism, or the Christian option which really works, a personal beginning.

This, of course, illuminates the tension that the unbeliever has in living in a world that belongs to God and reveals God, with a revelation even in himself of this God, yet denying the revelation. Schaeffer was building on the example of Paul in Athens (Acts 17:22-34) and in Lystra (Acts 14:15-17), and in Romans 1:19-20: 'For what can be known about God is plain to them, because God has shown it to them. For his invisible attributes, namely, his eternal power and divine nature, have been clearly perceived, ever since the creation of the world, in the things that have been made. So they are without excuse.'

One of the benefits of beginning with Creation is that one can take people back to their origins, not in the sense of having a debate about evolution, but in reminding them of their true identity. They are made in the image of God. This is more glorious than anything the atheist can conjure up. When one talks to a homosexual, for example, it means one is not only talking at the behavioural level of his breaking God's law (though that must be present), but getting him to consider what his identity is before God, created in God's image though a sinner. Evangelicals are often seen by the 'gay' community to offer only condemnation. Apologetics rooted in Creation may have something to contribute.

Second, he insists on the reality of the Fall. Schaeffer had a profound grasp of the reality of sin as it affects us intellectually, emotionally, physically and in the world around us. He grasped not only human guilt, but the tragedy of the Fall and how it affected not only the non-Christian, but the Christian who, in struggling to live the Christian life, would know real growth, but never perfect healing in this world.

Third, he seeks to expose the point of tension in the life of the person before him. This he calls 'taking the roof off' to expose the unbeliever, sometimes very painfully, to the inadequacy and nakedness of his worldview. This point may be at a philosophical level, such as how can you be sure anything really exists? It may be personal — how do you know you love your girlfriend or she you, if you proceed on a materialistic worldview? It may be ethical — if there is no God, what basis do you have for morals, other than instinct or pragmatism or the 51% vote? The 'New Atheists' make a lot of 'genocide' in the Bible. But apart from any other considerations, on what basis do they say genocide is wrong? The relativist has no firm place on which to stand to come to any firm conclusions about anything: either in metaphysics, to know that anything is really there; or in morals, to know what is right or wrong; or in epistemology, to know how one can know anything.

In other words, Schaeffer's apologetics is a matter of working out the implications of a biblical worldview, beginning with God, Creation and the Fall. It includes such basic rules of logic as that of non-contradiction, which has its origins in the fact that God exists as opposed to not existing. At some point there is inconsistency in the materialist's worldview, and he can only get along by borrowing from a theistic worldview, in fact a Christian one. To show where he is cheating by borrowing, and to point out the bankruptcy of his worldview in conjunction with establishing the viability of the Christian system, is the apologetic task.

A question sometimes asked is: does Schaeffer's apologetic approach work today, when people appear not to be worried about being inconsistent? This can be overstressed. Someone serious enough to engage in discussion of this nature is likely to be troubled by inconsistency if its consequences are carefully spelled out. One may also add that, first, no apologetic system 'works' just as a system. Schaeffer was the last person to want to rely on any technique. He focused on the person and always insisted on the need for the Holy Spirit to use any argument. Second, there have always been people who are not bothered by inconsistency. It is not a wholly new phenomenon. Third, a L'Abri worker, Dick Keyes, has found it more productive to talk about being 'dishonest' rather than inconsistent. Finally, Schaeffer would always say that when you have done all you can to reach people, the 'bottom line' is what Scripture says, not what the culture is: propositional truth must still be spoken into that culture. Some of the suggestions for 'further reading' are helpful in making further applications of Schaeffer's thought.

The following words on apologetics by F. F. Bruce, following a discussion of Acts 17:22-34, fit Schaeffer well:

> The twentieth century [and we may say, twenty-first century] apologist, in confronting contemporary paganism, especially in the western world, will find it necessary to expose erroneous ideas for what they are. He must remove obstacles which lie in the way of people's accepting the truth — false beliefs about God, for example. He must not try to accommodate the gospel to them, for all his endeavour to present it in an idiom understood by his hearers or readers. He will, however, be vigilant to seize upon every appropriate point of contact. Anything that rings a bell in his hearers' minds may serve, for their minds are full of questions and aspirations — sometimes only half-consciously realised — to which the answer and fulfilment are provided by the gospel'
> (*The Apostolic Defence of the Gospel* [IVF, 1959], p.41).

As has been said before, Schaeffer insisted that intellectual arguments were only part of the work. The final apologetic is love: the truth has to be spoken in love. For this reason Schaeffer was very cautious about debating with people publicly, as he was skilled enough to win, but his concern was to win people, not arguments. One debate he did enter, with Bishop James Pike in Chicago, was remembered by many, not for the fact that Schaeffer 'won', but because of the gentleness with which he dealt with his opponent. Bishop

Pike said he was the only debater to have treated him like a human being. Some have said Schaeffer was too gentle, in fact, but it led to a friendship which lasted till the bishop's death and opened the man's mind to at least listening to the gospel.

The unbeliever must be able to see love in action in the life of the Christians to whom he is speaking. Without such love our words will be the clanging of cymbals and the banging of gongs.

12

FILMS, POLITICS

AND THE FINAL BATTLE

Schaeffer had begun at L'Abri with intimate discussions, seminars and lectures. Then someone decided that the discussions were too good to be lost and began to tape them by hiding a microphone in a potted plant while a discussion was going on, much to Schaeffer's annoyance, though he soon became reconciled to the idea. After that, from the late sixties onwards, came the books. These were largely the fruit of lectures he had been giving for some years in America and the United Kingdom, with notable results: the books sold in millions, in twenty-five languages. We now enter a new phase of Schaeffer's influence, greater than anything seen so far and certainly more controversial: the making of films in the 1970s.

How Should We Then Live? appeared in 1976, having started life as a suggestion by Schaeffer's son, Franky, in July 1974. The idea was to trace, from a Christian perspective, the rise and decline of western thought and culture. In his note at the beginning of the book that accompanied the film series, Schaeffer calls it 'an analysis of the key moments in history which have formed our present culture, and the thinking of the people who brought those moments to pass'. Schaeffer was not entirely happy about working in the new medium, but was encouraged by a desire to answer the unfair treatment extended to the Reformation he felt the English scholar Kenneth Clark had given in his famous BBC TV series, *Civilisation*, and by reading Ezekiel 33:10 one morning during filming, from which the title came. It appealed to the Schaeffers that the producer of the film was Billy Zeoli, the son of the evangelist whom the young Fran had heard in Germantown in 1930.

The thesis of the film series is that of the trilogy, tracing western culture from Rome through the Middle Ages, the Renaissance, the Reformation, the Enlightenment, the rise of modern science, modern philosophy, art, music and literature, and analysing where we are today. Underlying his analysis, says Colin Duriez, is his 'threefold emphasis upon the lordship of Christ, the reliability and inerrancy of the Bible, and the necessity for a coherent Christian worldview'. Schaeffer expresses his fear at the end of the series that the loss of absolutes rooted in Scripture will lead to a totalitarianism of a new elite, and warns, in a way that seems strangely prescient today, of economic breakdown and democratic government being surrendered in favour of 'regimentation' as people fear instability more than the loss of freedom.

The series of ten episodes, incorporating visits to most of Europe's great museums, art galleries and historic monuments, was a considerable success, and the book, which is one of his best and well produced, sold well. Schaeffer went on a twenty-two-city seminar tour to introduce the series. He spoke to 6,600 in Los Angeles, 3,900 in Chicago, and 4,400 in Toronto. It made a considerable impact on evangelical Christians on both sides of the Atlantic, perhaps more in America than in Britain — some British Christians never quite got beyond the goatee beard and knee-breeches! It is difficult to appreciate today, when Christians (in considerable measure due to his example and teaching) are much more involved in politics, the arts and general culture, just how ground-breaking his work was.

The closing chapters mention *Roe v Wade*, the United States Supreme Court ruling of January 1973 which (with a companion case, *Doe v Bolton*) conferred on women in the US a right to abortion up to the point of 'viability' (about twenty-eight weeks) but in practice to full term if the mother's health, including mental health and well-being, are adjudged to be at risk. Schaeffer called this a 'totally arbitrary absolute' both medically in terms of the time-limit and legally as an exercise in judicial law-making. A meeting at Huémoz in 1977 with the Christian surgeon and family friend C. Everett Koop, with considerable encouragement again from Franky, increased the momentum for the film series that would be called *Whatever Happened To The Human Race?* The main thesis is that relativism has inevitably led to loss of respect for human life, as witnessed in the 'abortion on demand' ruling of *Roe v Wade*. The real danger, as well as the documented practice, of infanticide was highlighted, as well as euthanasia as 'the next logical step'. Schaeffer sets out the biblical basis for human dignity and exhorts Christians in these words: 'On the basis of an unweakened Bible, we must teach and act, in our individual lives and as citizens, on the fact that every individual has unique value as made in the image of God.' It is a question of acknowledging the Lordship of Christ over all of life. 'Every person is worth fighting for.' He takes personhood back to the point of conception.

The attendances at the promotional seminars for this film series were smaller. Many evangelicals were uncomfortable about being told to get up and *do* something about abortion. Schaeffer was not only speaking to evangelicals, though. He believed that on these moral issues it was right to work with others with whom he was not in doctrinal agreement. He was happy to stand alongside a Roman Catholic or a Mormon. He distinguished such 'co-belligerents' from an 'ally': 'An ally is a person who is a born-again Christian with whom I can go a long way down the road... A co-belligerent is a person who may not have any sufficient basis for taking the right position but takes the right position on a single issue' (Martin Wroe and Dave Roberts, *Adrift in the 80s: the Strait Interviews*, ed. Stewart Henderson [Marshall Morgan and Scott, 1986], p.31, cited in Duriez, p.192). He would work with the co-belligerent on the single issue but no further.

In 1981 *A Christian Manifesto* was published, in which Schaeffer called for Christians to be prepared for civil disobedience in upholding God's law. He particularly had in mind the protection of the unborn child, the elderly and the weak. He insisted that the state must be subject to the law of God and drew on the writings of Reformers like John Knox (*c.* 1513–1572) and Puritans such as Samuel Rutherford (1600–1661), who in *Lex, Rex* ('The Law is King', as Schaeffer translated it) argued that all monarchs are subject to the law and not a law to themselves. God is over Caesar, and when any office commands what is contrary to God's law, it abrogates its authority, argued Schaeffer. Let it be clear, he was not advocating violence, but the withholding of taxes and other means of passive civil disobedience. It is, of course, true that there comes a point when every Christian must obey God rather than man, but not everyone found Schaeffer's thesis in this book convincing.

Schaeffer has probably come under more criticism for the political involvement into which the 'pro-life' film series and writings brought him than for anything else. Such criticism has varied from those who think he just got absorbed in politics to the detriment of his evangelism, to those who disliked the fact that he worked with (if only as a 'co-belligerent') Roman Catholics; or that he was closely allied to and a primary thinker for the American 'Right' and the 'Moral Majority'. After all, he did say in *A Christian Manifesto* that he thought the election of the pro-life President Reagan was an open window for rolling back the 'material-energy, chance world view'. Some have even argued that there are 'three Schaeffers': the early fundamentalist, the open-minded European, then a reversion to American fundamentalist again in his last years.

The truth is that Schaeffer saw doing what he could to change the law as it stood after *Roe v Wade* as his simple duty as a Christian. If all things are under the Lordship of Christ, shouldn't I as a Christian seek to obey God in every area and seek to have God's laws honoured in every area of life? Why should politics be a 'no-go' area for Christians any more than art, music, literature or philosophy — Christian involvement in which Schaeffer had championed throughout his ministry? Indeed, in view of the greater issues hanging on political activity, it is even more important to have Christians involved. It was no more than love of neighbour. He had a life-long dislike of 'pietism', and in *A Christian Manifesto* he explains what he means by this. Pietism began in the seventeenth century as a healthy protest against formal, dry Christianity, but it made too sharp a division between the spiritual and the material world — a division Schaeffer calls 'platonic'. 'The totality of human existence was not afforded a proper place. In particular it neglected the intellectual dimension of Christianity.' Schaeffer was all for what we would call 'experiential' Christianity in that it is not just a set of doctrines, but he insisted too that Christ's Lordship covers all areas of life and nothing concerning reality is excluded. Even if one does not agree with everything he wrote or did, there can be no serious denial of his integrity and the consistency of the work of his last years with all that had gone before.

There can be no denying, either, the impact his work had on evangelicals, particularly in America. Franky Schaeffer was probably right when he wrote:

> The impact of our two film series, as well as their companion books, was to give the evangelical community a frame of reference through which to understand the secularization of American culture, and to point to the 'human life issue' as the watershed between a 'Christian society' and a utilitarian relativistic 'post-Christian' future stripped of compassion and beauty
>
> (*Crazy for God*, p.273).

As late as 1997 Schaeffer was described in *Christianity Today* as 'evangelicalism's most important public intellectual' who 'prodded evangelicals out of their cultural ghettoes'. Yet Schaeffer insisted that Americans must not confuse the kingdom of God with the nation of America or 'wrap Christianity in the national flag'.

Indirect echoes of Schaeffer's analysis of our culture may be found in unexpected places. This comment on a proposal by an English city to use the burning of corpses in crematoria to generate electricity appeared recently on an atheist 'blog':

> Who's the atheist here? It's me remember? So why is it that I'm having to defend the sanctity of human life? We all know that the future Hitler planned to impose on us is now just around the corner through our own free choice, and be-tween the abortions at one end and the euthanasia at the other — not compulsory, you understand, merely encour-aged with all the 24 hour blanket subtlety the media class can muster — we will soon have a good twenty years or so ... before our bags are packed for us, provided we're perfect in the first place of course. Or what passes for perfect these days: incredibly uninformed and fashionably dressed. I don't believe in pixies and elves but I do know ideas have conse-quences, and that pragmatism in matters once deemed spir-itual — the application to social policy of the Darwinian fact that we are evolved animals that invented morality — leads to a kind of universal Auschwitz where there is no purpose to living and so no right to it, without the consent of a coun-cil of technocratic bigots wearing Richard Dawkins masks.
>
> (http://venerablebeads.blogspot.com/2011/12/
> nothing-special.html).

I believe Schaeffer would have said, 'He understands; he really understands'.

It was towards the end of filming *Whatever Happened to the Human Race?* in August 1978 that it was noticed that Schaeffer's coat was much too large for him. Weight loss had been dramatic. He was taken to the Mayo Clinic in Rochester, Minnesota, and discovered to have a tumour the size of a football as a result of lymphoma. Chemotherapy began on 17 October. By the following March he was in remission and able to travel, and even took part in a pro-life rally in Hyde Park with John Stott and Malcolm Muggeridge. The period of treatment was also not wasted. He tells of how doctors at the Mayo Clinic asked him to speak at *How Should We Then Live?* seminars. A Rochester branch of L'Abri was started and became the American headquarters. A L'Abri Conference was held there in 1980. He went back to Switzerland, which he regarded as home, and carried on life as normally as possible. He revised the *Complete Works* edition of his writings by 1982.

We can be grateful that he was given energy enough to write one more book, although most of the work on the manuscript was done by Lane Dennis of Crossway Books. *The Great Evangelical Disaster* was published in early 1984, just months before his death; and though he had been very ill throughout late 1983 and early 1984, he mustered enough strength to complete a thirteen-city tour to lecture on the theme of the book:

We as Bible-believing evangelical Christians are locked in a battle. This is not a friendly gentleman's discussion. It is a life and death conflict between the spiritual hosts of wickedness and those who claim the name of Christ... Here is the great evangelical disaster — the failure of the evangelical world to stand for truth as truth. There is only one word for this — accommodation... Evangelicals are facing a watershed concerning the nature of biblical inspiration and authority.

It was fitting that Schaeffer's last work should be a heartfelt cry for a strong stand on the inerrancy of the Book on which his whole ministry had been based. What we need, he concluded, is 'a generation of radicals for truth and for Christ. We need a young generation who will be willing to stand in loving confrontation, but real confrontation, in contrast to the mentality of constant accommodation with the current forms of the world spirit...'

The Lord for whom he had lived and fought took him into his presence on 15 May 1984. Edith wrote in a letter that his last breath was taken at 4.00 am precisely,

> ...and he was absent. That absence was so sharp and so precise. Absent! ...As for his presence with the Lord, I had to turn to my Bible to know that. I only know that a person is present with the Lord because the Bible tells us so. I did not have a mystical experience... My husband fought for truth and fought for the truth of the inspiration of the Bible — the inerrancy of the Bible — all the 52 years that I knew him. But never have I been more impressed with the wonder of having a trustworthy message from God, an unshakable word from God, than right then!
>
> *(Dear Family, The L'Abri Family Letters, 1961–86* [Harper and Row, 1989], pp.388-9).

13

SCHAEFFER'S LEGACY

The doctrine of Creation

The greatest contribution Schaeffer made to Christian thinking was to emphasize the doctrine of Creation and apply it in apologetics and in sanctification. It is a doctrine that, when evangelicalism is under the kind of pressure to which the Fundamentalists were responding, can get lost. The focus comes to rest on issues of redemption and a narrow view of what the Christian life involves. A negative attitude towards the world and a form of legalism can result, which detrimentally affects both our evangelism and our Christian living. 'We always should realize, and I cannot say it often enough, that Christianity is a creation-centred teaching.'

Closely allied to this is the fact that 'God is systematic in His creation and revelation.' By holding firmly to the system of biblical revelation and applying it to the issues of his day, Schaeffer achieved tremendous intellectual penetration which made much of his analysis prophetic.

1. In apologetics

It was his grasp of the fact that all men and women are made in the image of God and live in God's world, and also that there is a revelation of God in their 'mannishness' and in the form of the cosmos, that enabled him to discern the realities both of 'common' (but not neutral) ground with unbelievers, and also of the 'point of tension' to which the unbeliever needs to be pushed as 'the roof' is taken off his inadequate worldview. In addition, Schaeffer's viewpoint enabled him to tackle the unbeliever's sin, not just as a moral issue against God's law, but as a wholesale assault on his own identity as a human being, and, thereby, on his Creator in whose image he had been created.

2. In sanctification

'The Lordship of Christ in all of life' was the unifying theme of Schaeffer's teaching, with obvious implications for the Christian. Because of his grasp of this world as God's creation, however, sanctification as obeying Christ is not making forays into an alien environment, but walking firmly where Christ is already Lord. What is to be feared is not creation, 'For everything created by God is good, and nothing is to be rejected if it is received with thanksgiving' (1 Tim. 4:4), but sin. In this, Schaeffer was very much of one mind with Abraham Kuyper, who insisted that 'In the total expanse of human life there is not a single square inch of which Christ, who alone is sovereign, does not declare, "That is mine!"'

This enabled him to encourage Christians to get involved in areas of life where the fundamentalism out of which he had come was very wary. Christians, taught Schaeffer, could be philosophers. Paul's words in 1 Corinthians 1:18 – 2:16 and Colossians 2:8 have sometimes been used to suggest that all philosophy is dangerous for a Christian. Paul's target, however, is the rationalist autonomy of the mind, not the use of the mind submitted to Scripture. One of Schaeffer's great contributions was to embrace philosophical issues and questions within a biblical theological worldview. Many people who were not finding answers to genuine questions in their churches, or were being told not to ask questions because that was unspiritual, or who found that they could make no real connection between the teaching of their evangelical churches and the intellectual problems their friends outside had, were profoundly grateful to Schaeffer. He warned of the dangers of Christians being told, 'Don't question, just believe', of loading too much on 'the donkey of devotion', whose back would eventually break and faith would collapse. Ultimately, we need reasons for faith; the mind must be satisfied. Scripture gives us that. Of course, it goes beyond what our minds can grasp, but it is never less than intellectually satisfying.

This was my personal experience of Schaeffer's teaching. A rather dissatisfied evangelical, never really given answers in church to the questions I had, or able to make satisfying connections between my Christian life and the world outside the church, I was hungry for the Bible-based answers Schaeffer gave — at least as much in his sermons as in his 'philosophical' works. One effect on me was to cause me to read Calvin's *Institutes* in the year after meeting him, and go on to the works of Dr Lloyd-Jones and the Puritans. Schaeffer, supplemented by frequent visits to L'Abri in Greatham, Hampshire, introduced me, in short, to the riches of Reformed theology.

In the same way, Christians could get involved in psychology, though it would be a struggle in college, and their presuppositions would be very different from the fundamental tenets of the discipline. Christians could also be artists. What is Christian art? Jerram Barrs says it is 'art that is produced by a Christian'. Christian art may be about the cross or a redemptive subject; but equally it may be about anything in creation, because God is the Lord of all creation. 'Christian' art, music or literature does not have to be about redemption. But as a Christian artist produces a body of work, his/her worldview and presuppositions will slowly be revealed. And as we have seen, Christians can get involved in politics, remembering that Calvin called the work of the 'magistrate', 'the most sacred of callings'.

In all this, Schaeffer never downplayed the centrality of Christ's redemptive work. He was firmly convinced of the historic Fall. Unbelievers needed the finished work of Christ to be forgiven their sins, and true spirituality in the Christian life meant living day by day on the basis of the finished work of Christ. 'Healing' in this life could never be more than 'substantial', but, by God's grace through Christ's blood, it could be that. Read his sermons, or *True Spirituality*, or his letters, to be convinced of that (though these truths are present in his more philosophical works as well).

The life of the mind

Schaeffer is wrongly called a rationalist, as should be clear, but he was convinced that Christianity is rational, for God is a rational God. One of Schaeffer's favourite texts was 'As he thinketh in his heart, so is he' (Proverbs 23:7, KJV, translated differently in modern versions). This was a valuable emphasis in the 1960s and 1970s, not only against the neo-orthodoxy which he called 'semantic mysticism', but against the burgeoning charismatic movement which downgraded the mind in favour of 'experience'. The teaching of L'Abri on charismatic issues was immensely helpful to many young Christians in the 1980s. It is still important in our postmodern (or post-postmodern) days. Christianity is still 'true Truth' about all of life, and Christians must guard against a creeping anti-intellectualism imbibed from the culture. Truth may be more than propositional, but it is never less. One of the characteristics of life 'below the line of despair' is indifference to the pursuit of truth because we don't believe it is there to be found. Christians catch this indifference. The apostle Paul, however, insisted that 'We destroy arguments and every lofty opinion raised against the knowledge of God, and take every thought captive to obey Christ' (2 Cor. 10:5). Prayer, authentic living and *persuasion* — these are the elements of effective evangelism.

The importance of living the truth

The 1951 turning point in Schaeffer's life came when he questioned the reality of his own Christian life and the danger in the 'separated movement' of losing touch with real spirituality. He and Edith insisted that prayer would be central in their lives and in the life of L'Abri. L'Abri was not to be a 'discussion' or 'teaching' centre only, but a demonstration that God exists. In his works on the life of the church (*The Church at the End of the Twentieth Century*, *The Church Before the Watching World* and *The Mark of the Christian*), he is insistent on the demonstration of love in the Christian life. It is the 'final apologetic' by which the world will know we are Jesus' disciples (John 13:35) and will know that the Father sent the Son (John 17:23). Schaeffer displayed this in his personal attention to individuals, in his attentive listening and in his energy-draining sacrifices, whether on behalf of the unborn child or the inerrancy of Scripture, in the last years of his life. Together, he and Edith displayed love in the sacrificial use of their home at L'Abri. We hear much today of the importance of 'community' and 'relationships' in giving our evangelism credibility. Schaeffer was already there.

Christian involvement in public life

Many Christians who have become involved in politics and public life in the last four decades would acknowledge that Schaeffer was an influence. He painfully aroused evangelicals to their duty in issues of the protection of the unborn child and of infanticide and euthanasia. His great strength was that these were not merely 'moral' campaigns, but by rooting what he said in the nature of humans as created and in his analysis of western thought, he showed us *why* life, from conception on, should be protected, and the real moral horror of the intellectual vacuum in the west. His influence got evangelicals going in providing care for unmarried mothers as well as in political campaigning, and it is interesting to see today more discussion about the importance of Christian involvement in politics. Will this save people? No, of course not — Schaeffer never pretended it would — but there is no incompatibility between preaching the gospel and political involvement.

A powerful example of Christian influence in public life is the work of Vishal Mangalwadi in India who, inspired by Schaeffer's teaching, courageously and sacrificially stood up for poor farmers against oppression and institutional apathy. His is a potent illustration of the way Christian thinking about the identity of the individual makes a difference as opposed to, say, the Hindu concept of reality. His story is told briefly in *Francis A. Schaeffer: Portraits of the man and his work.*

The inerrancy of Scripture

The final issue for which Christians should be profoundly grateful is Schaeffer's sterling defence of the inerrancy of Scripture. *The Great Evangelical Disaster* is a book all Christians, or at least all ministers, should read and heed. In 1977 he was involved in setting up the International Council on Biblical Inerrancy. 'His sense of both the greatness and tragedy of human life pervaded everything he said, as did the corresponding sense that God has spoken and has given us truth which is unshakable' (David Wells, commending *Francis Schaeffer: A Mind and Heart for God*).

Conclusion

Francis Schaeffer had many critics. He was criticized for his supposedly superficial scholarship; for creating a distraction from evangelism by his concentration on culture; for being too involved, in his later years, in politics and, in particular, being too close to the 'Christian Right' and the

Moral Majority; for wearing knee-breeches and having a funny beard (though as to the 'knickers', as Americans call them, Edith said he wore those simply because in the Alps he was comfortable in them and never saw much need to change when he went abroad); for being too intellectual and philosophical and rationalizing the faith; and so on. Perhaps the most hurtful criticisms have come in more recent years from the semi-autobiographical writings of his son, Franky. Franky turned his back on evangelicalism in 1990, joining the Greek Orthodox Church. He has recently gone on record as calling religion 'dumb' and the Bible a 'fraud'. His real spleen is vented against the American Right, which he is conscious of having had a hand in founding. He has adopted the policy of purging his own conscience by confessing his parents' sins and has said hurtful things that need to be read in the context of the life of Schaeffer as thousands knew him, including those who were very close to him and Edith.

The criticisms (or at least some of them) and the discussion will doubtless go on. 'For many in the 1960s', writes Os Guinness, 'Francis Schaeffer was the great door opener — opening the door to regaining the lordship of Christ over the whole of life and culture. For me personally, he stood head and shoulders above most others because of the way he took God so seriously, people so seriously, and truth so seriously. A flawed human being as we all are, he was a giant of the faith to whom we owe more than many people realise' (*Francis Schaeffer: A Mind and Heart for God*, p.viii). As we review the life of this remarkable man, we may call him a prophet for his prescient analysis of trends in philosophy that explain where we are today; we may call him an apologist; less accurately, though popular articles and publishers' blurbs delight in it, he may be called a philosopher. Fundamentally though, Francis Schaeffer rejoiced in being a pastor and evangelist. That is how he began and, through many twists and turns, that is what he remained to the end.

FURTHER READING

Schaeffer's life

The most accessible biography, and highly recommended, is Colin Duriez' *Francis Schaeffer: An Authentic Life* (IVP, 2008). I am hugely indebted to this work. Edith Schaeffer's *The Tapestry* (Word Books 1981, Special Memorial Edition 1984) is the indispensable detailed account of the Schaeffers' lives. Edith wrote specifically about the founding of L'Abri in *L'Abri* (Norfolk Press, 1969). Jerram Barrs' *Francis Schaeffer: The Early Years* and *The Later Years*, two sets of lectures from Covenant Seminary Worldwide Classroom, 1989–1990, are also full of helpful material.

Schaeffer's works

The five-volume *The Complete Works of Francis Schaeffer* (Crossway Books, 1982) contains all twenty-two of Schaeffer's major writings. A number of his works can be obtained individually.

Schaeffer's ideas

These are well expounded by Ranald Macaulay and Jerram
Barrs in *Being Human — the nature of spiritual experience*
(Inter Varsity, 1978, reprinted in England by Solway, 1996).
Francis A. Schaeffer: Portraits of the Man and his Work
(ed. Lane T. Dennis, Crossway Books, 1986) contains
excellent essays, sympathetically critical, and testimonies
to his ministry. *Reflections on Francis Schaeffer* (ed. Ronald
Ruegsegger, Academie Books, 1986) provides some rigorous
discussion of Schaeffer, including less sympathetic but
very useful critiques, and a superb pen-portrait by J. I.
Packer. *Letters of Francis A. Schaeffer* (ed. Lane T. Dennis,
Crossway Books, 1985) reveals Schaeffer's pastoral heart.
His apologetics is discussed in *Truth With Love — the
apologetics of Francis Schaeffer* (Bryan A. Follis, Crossway
Books, 2006). Nancy Pearcey's *Total Truth* (Crossway,
2004, 2005) is a wide-ranging extension and application of
Schaeffer's thought to a more contemporary scene. *Francis
Schaeffer: A Mind and Heart for God* (ed. Bruce A. Little,
P&R, 2010) contains five helpful essays on Schaeffer and his
current relevance. Schaeffer would also have enjoyed Vishal
Mangalwadi's *The Book That Made Your World* (Thomas
Nelson, 2011) on the biblical foundation of Western culture.

L'Abri

Web sites: www.labri.org;
for a wealth of useful lectures including many by Schaeffer
visit www.labri-ideas-library.org.